EVERYONE IS PSYCHIC

Discover the Edgar Cayce way to developing your psychic self...

...and learn the secret power of such psychic phenomena as

**AURAS * MEDITATION * TELEPATHY
VISUALIZATION * COLORS * DIET
ASTROLOGY * PAST LIVES
DREAMS * CHANNELING * KARMA
SPIRIT GUIDES * SÉANCES * HEALTH**

EVERYONE IS PSYCHIC

*The Edgar Cayce Way
to Unlock Your Own Hidden Psychic Ability
for a Richer, More Rewarding Life*

ELIZABETH FULLER

FOREWORD BY CHARLES THOMAS CAYCE,
PRESIDENT OF THE ASSOCIATION
FOR RESEARCH AND ENLIGHTENMENT

BERKLEY BOOKS, NEW YORK

Grateful acknowledgment is hereby given to the following source for permission to reprint the material listed below:

''The Road Not Taken'' by Robert Frost, from *The Poetry of Robert Frost*,
copyright © 1975 by Henry Holt and Company, Inc. Used by permission.

This Berkley book contains the complete text of the original hardcover
edition. It has been completely reset in a typeface designed for easy reading
and was printed from new film.

EVERYONE IS PSYCHIC

A Berkley Book / published by arrangement with
Crown Publishers, Inc.

PRINTING HISTORY
Crown edition published 1989
Berkley edition / October 1990

ISBN: 0-425-12303-0

A BERKLEY BOOK ® TM 757,375
Berkley Books are published by The Berkley Publishing Group,
200 Madison Avenue, New York, New York 10016.
The name ''Berkley'' and the ''B'' logo
are trademarks belonging to Berkley Publishing Corporation.

PRINTED IN THE UNITED STATES OF AMERICA
10 9 8 7 6 5 4 3 2 1

For John and Christopher

CONTENTS

FOREWORD

Throughout his life my grandfather expressed his conviction that everyone is psychic, although often such ability lies latent and unobserved. Edgar Cayce was also firm in stating that with proper and careful development our psychic ability could enhance virtually every aspect of our lives, providing us with a deeper understanding of life and its true purpose. He made it plain that we were not to think of the psychic as mysterious but as a natural part of us—an extension of our five senses.

I am pleased that Elizabeth Fuller has so carefully brought together my grandfather's methods and suggestions for unlocking psychic ability within all of us, as well as his thoughts concerning how such ability can be utilized for constructive and creative living. I am sure the reader will find the book delightfully readable as well as enlightening and useful.

CHARLES THOMAS CAYCE

Every entity has clairvoyant,
mystic, psychic powers.
—Edgar Cayce

INTRODUCTION

The wind was whipping in off the stormy Atlantic when I arrived at a beach-front hotel in Virginia Beach. It was nearly midnight on a raw March evening in 1987. I had left Westport, Connecticut, that morning for a ten-hour train ride. Physically I felt as if I had dismounted from the Dead Gulch Stage Coach. Mentally I was buoyed by the prospects that lay ahead.

As the taxi driver handed me my change, he asked what in the world I was doing in Virginia Beach this chilled time of the year. I told him that I was here to research the work of Edgar Cayce at the headquarters down the road. The driver shrugged his shoulders New York style and said, "I should have known. In the last year I've taken more people to that Cayce place than anywhere else." Then he looked at his meter and called out the window, "One day I'm going to go over there and check out that Cayce guy!"

What about this man Cayce? The *New York Times*, one of the world's more cautious publications, discovered Cayce back in October 1910. The headline read: ILLITERATE MAN

BECOMES DOCTOR WHEN HYPNOTIZED. Subheads went on to say: Psychist Diagnoses and Cures Patients. Ignorant of Medicine, He Turns Healer in Trance . . . Strange Power Shown by Edgar Cayce Puzzles Physicians . . . Physician Says Kentucky Man Has Wonderful Powers . . . Remarkable and Successful Treatments Are Sworn To in Affadavits . . . Psychic Power New to Medical World . . .

This was only the beginning. Edgar Cayce's paranormal powers were not limited to the medical. The scope of his cosmic treasury was as boundless as the universe he examined and interpreted. While in a trance state he provided penetrating insights into the mysteries of the body, mind, and soul.

By 1930, Edgar Cayce was the Western world's answer to the gurus of the East. Dubbed by the media "The Sleeping Prophet," he lay on a couch and allowed himself to be put in a trance. People seeking help from serious illness, deep emotional or mental disturbances, or everyday frustrations wrote him. Their questions were read to Cayce while he was in an altered state of consciousness. All he needed to know was the name and address of the inquirer. Then he announced, "Yes, we have the body here."

In a strange, inexplicable way he visualized the disorder. Then he diagnosed and prescribed treatments in detail. Often Cayce felt the presence of the distant person so vividly that he could describe everything from what the person was wearing to his activities, from brushing his teeth to tying his shoelaces.

If Cayce were dealing with a medical case, he displayed vast knowledge of medical science, although he had received no formal education beyond the sixth grade. To the conventional medical mind this seemed almost impossible. As one irritated doctor put it: "Why the hell should I spend all these years in medical school if some illiterate can lie on his couch with his eyes closed and prescribe better than I or any other trained doctor?'' Yet this elementary-school drop-out repeatedly proved from the early 1900s until his death in 1945 that he could perform wonders.

All this was accomplished during times when people considered the psychic to be very low-grade merchandise. This is not to say that there was any great heightened awareness when I was growing up in the fifties in Cleveland Heights. Emblazoned on my memory was the time Aunt Betty blurted out at dinner that she had seen the angels take her grandmother away. It was hard to discern how far the eyeballs around the table rolled back in their sockets. My uncle Bud, a U.S. marshal, mumbled something about bringing out the handcuffs. My father snapped, ''Get the net!'' My cousins and brother whooped, booed, and hooted.

I thought back on this family scene as I checked into the hotel in Virginia Beach. A pleasant young man with a soft Southern drawl handed me my room key along with an envelope. Inside was a note from Charles Thomas Cayce, Edgar Cayce's grandson, the president of the Association for Research and Enlightenment, an organization formed to carry out his grandfather's life, work, and principles. The note read:

Dear Elizabeth:

We are enthusiastic about the plans for your new book on my grandfather. As I mentioned to you on the phone, people everywhere have written us that they have felt personal signs of incipient psychic ability that seem to arise spontaneously. They are eager to understand and develop this. Since my grandfather has spoken at length on this subject, I'm sure such a book as you propose will be important and widely helpful. We will be glad to assist you in every way.

Also in the envelope was a detailed agenda for my visit. It was packed with a schedule of lunches, meetings, lectures, and dinners. The next evening, in fact, I would be having dinner at Charles Thomas's home. Such gracious cooperation was welcome. For me to interpret the impressive background material on Edgar Cayce's methods for developing psychic ability, I would need expert guidance, which grandson Charles Thomas was soon to provide.

The morning after my arrival, I got up rested and refreshed. After I checked my tape recorder and made a few notes, I went down to the hotel dining room, which overlooked the Atlantic. There was a heavy spray whipping off the top of the breakers, adding to the mystical atmosphere. As I ate breakfast, I tried to imagine Virginia Beach back in the 1930s and '40s when Edgar Cayce was giving psychic readings in a building across the street from where I was seated. Although Cayce had been dead for over forty years, I couldn't shake the feeling that his presence permeated the surroundings. Perhaps it was just the anticipation of what I was to discover in my quest. Or perhaps it was because in the previous month I had read all I could about Cayce and was steeped in wonderment.

Bending against the March wind, I made my way across broad Atlantic Avenue and down a dozen or so blocks to the Association for Research and Enlightenment, known as the A.R.E. My first scheduled appointment was a nine o'clock meeting with Charles Thomas Cayce.

The Cayce complex is impressive. There are two buildings within a hundred yards of each other. The new one is clean, white, and contemporary. The other structure sits behind it on a hill with a sweeping view of the Atlantic. It's an older, rambling white frame building that looks more like a gracious country estate than the former hospital where Cayce's treatments had been administered in earlier years.

Today, however, it houses offices for the A.R.E.

My meeting was in the modern building. It contains the expansive library, two auditoriums, staff offices, and two serene meditation rooms. The lobby is on the first floor. On the left is a portrait of Edgar Cayce with his wife, Gertrude. Beneath the painting is a slide projector that gives a mini-presentation of the life and work of Edgar Cayce. I was a few minutes early, so I sat and watched the capsule version of his life.

I had forgotten that when Edgar Cayce was a small child he was able to see his dead relatives. He also had the uncanny ability to fall asleep with a schoolbook under his head and awake with perfect recall of the text without having even opened the book. This was somewhat disconcerting for his parents, church-going folks who lived on a small farm in Hopkinsville, Kentucky, at the turn of the century. These were the first signs of his burgeoning psychic ability that would later startle the world.

Charles Thomas was not at all how I had imagined he would be. I had read so much about his grandfather that I had just assumed he might radiate some of the homespun flavor of his grandfather, but there was none I could detect. Charles Thomas is tall, distinguished, and a boyish forty-five. He spoke with the fluency of a college professor and the warmth of an old friend.

"Liz," he said as he greeted me at the door of his office, "we're all enthusiastic about your book project!"

I told him that I felt privileged to work on a book that would put Edgar Cayce's profound insights on psychic development to practical use. I also told Charles Thomas that the anticipation of entering into the vast Cayce archives made me feel as if I was about to plunge into a metaphysical whirlpool that would relax and stimulate at the same time.

Charles Thomas smiled and said, "I think my grandfather

might have thought of the Atlantic Ocean across the street as a metaphysical whirlpool.''

Charles Thomas spoke casually about the thousands of A.R.E. members who had joined because their own formerly hidden psychic tendencies had emerged without warning.

"This happens to an unusually large percentage of people," he said as he leaned back in a heavy leather chair. "Small signs appear spontaneously: sharp hunches or intuitions that turn out to be surprisingly accurate."

Charles Thomas ruffled through a stack of mail on his oak desk. "Here's a recent survey that points up the current wide-spread belief in the paranormal," he said. He passed the survey to me.

The survey was conducted by Father Andrew Greeley of the University of Chicago National Opinion Research Center. Although Father Greeley is a Catholic priest and sociologist, he is best known as a popular novelist. Based on a sampling of 1,470 people, the poll concluded that 67 percent of Americans now profess a belief in the supernatural. This is up from 58 percent in 1973. Twenty-nine percent believe in reincarnation or have had a psychic experience. And 42 percent believe they have been in communication with someone deceased.

I told Charles Thomas that I was surprised the statistics were so high. He said that he was a bit surprised too. But then he went on to say that after Shirley MacLaine's television miniseries depicted her own psychic experiences, the A.R.E. was bombarded with inquiries. Membership went up by one-third in a single month. He said that he felt this increase resulted from people who saw the TV series and suddenly realized they weren't alone with their paranormal experiences.

"You must occasionally get letters from loonies who say

they're hearing voices telling them to do something," I said.

"Oh sure," Charles Thomas said. "But we're not trying to play psychiatrist. We just present Edgar Cayce's deep conviction: Turn yourself over to the Creative Source that put us here in the first place. Anyone might be helped."

"Do people send in letters even if they haven't had any psychic experiences?"

"Yes, plenty of them. But most write because they or people close to them have had surprising psychic experiences. They're interested in further understanding these happenings."

I told him about my husband, John, who as a journalist became very interested in the whole paranormal field and has even written several books on it. But on a personal level he doesn't seem to allow himself to have a direct experience. In fact, he boasts that he's so bad at seeing the future that in 1940 he bet ten dollars that there would never be network TV. In 1950 he bet another ten bucks that there would never be color TV. In 1960 he bet twenty-five that a man would never walk on the moon.

"Maybe John didn't want to run Jeane Dixon out of town," Charles Thomas said with an engaging half-smile. Then he added, "Actually I can relate to John."

"How do you mean?" I asked.

"For a long time I resisted allowing myself to experience anything that might be termed 'psychic.' Just as John probably doesn't like to take off his investigative journalist's hat, I didn't want to remove my psychologist's hat."

"Because of your grandfather?" I asked.

"That's probably the main reason. I remember as a kid I was bodysurfing down at the beach with a bunch of neighborhood kids. They began taunting me, saying things like, 'Your father works at the Spook House on the hill.' That had a big impact on me."

I interrupted to say: "So instead of joining the 'house on the hill', you opted to become a child psychologist?"

"Exactly."

"How did you finally become involved in the A.R.E.?" I asked.

"I began working as a child psychologist at the A.R.E. children's camp. Shortly after that, I began to study Edgar Cayce's readings on children. And from there I began working with children who had psychic ability. Then in 1970 I took over the president's job from my father, Hugh Lynn Cayce. He had had a heart attack and had to shift responsibilities."

When Charles Thomas mentioned that he had worked with children who had psychic ability, I recalled an interesting case he had written about in the A.R.E. monthly magazine, *Venture Inward*. In his column, "President's Message," Charles Thomas wrote about a young girl whom he had met while he was the head of the youth activities program. Phyllis was a fourteen-year-old child who showed extraordinary psychic ability. I asked Charles Thomas about her. He went on to say:

"Phyllis came to my attention because her junior high school teacher and her parents were concerned. Her father, indeed, was quite angry, because Phyllis insisted that she had a playmate named Phil whom no one else could see. Children frequently talk about imaginary playmates, but seldom after they reach the age of fourteen. It's not surprising that her family was alarmed.

"Phyllis told me that her imaginary playmate, Phil, had died suddenly, not long before she became acquainted with him. He refused to tell her where he had died or his last name. I asked if I might speak with Phil. She thought for a moment and said no. But later she said that if I wanted to question Phil, she would relay my questions to him and tell me his answers.

"As a result, I conducted an experiment. I went down the hall to another office, opened a book, and left it open on a desk while I returned to the room where Phyllis waited. I suggested that she ask Phil the page number that showed on the open book. She paused, then said a number. I returned to the other room and confirmed that the number she gave was correct.

"We repeated the experiment a dozen times with different pages open. I even laid the book upside down so no one could see the page at which it was open. Phyllis—or Phil— was correct every time."

Charles Thomas continued, "I was never able to determine clearly whether Phil was a discarnate entity or simply a symbol for Phyllis's own psychic ability. But the experience showed me some ways in which we might help children who have such extraordinary experiences."

"Mind if I ask a personal question?" I said.

"Depends on how personal," Charles Thomas answered with a chuckle.

"Do you have any of your grandfather's special powers?"

"If you mean can I lie on a sofa and give a trance reading for a little old lady in Keokuk, Iowa, no. But I use my psychic ability for other things."

"For instance?"

"Let's see," Charles Thomas began, "just the other night I had been talking to my wife about a recurring dream. It turned out that the dream was able to provide valuable insight into our relationship."

"In what way?" I asked.

"Well, the dream was a way of opening up discussion about a particular situation that we hadn't even been consciously aware of. Once we were made aware of it, we could deal with it effectively."

Charles Thomas went on to say that in addition to dreams, he uses daily meditation.

"Meditation is the greatest way to open your psychic channel." As my grandfather said, "It is listening to the Divine within."

At this point Charles Thomas told a whimsical but practical way that meditation had come in handy only weeks earlier. He had been at home packing for a weekend seminar when he suddenly realized that all of his slacks were at the dry cleaner. His wife, Leslie, told him to pick them up on the way to the airport. But when he got to the dry cleaner he was informed that he needed his ticket. The cleaners had just modernized their system and a ticket number was the only way to locate his slacks. At first, Charles Thomas said, he panicked. But then he went to a quiet corner and meditated on the number. A few moments later he said to the clerk, "Try number 177." Within second he was handed his slacks.

"Did you mention to the clerk how you came up with the number?" I asked.

"When you have the last name of Cayce, you don't want to push it!" He laughed, then went on, "I think that at least every week we use health suggestions in our family. This isn't very dramatic, but about a month ago my daughter got a plantar wart on her foot, and we rubbed Edgar Cayce's home remedy of castor oil and baking soda on it."

"And it went away?" I asked.

"It did," he said, adding, "during the treatment we kept reminding her to refer to it not as 'her wart' but as 'the wart.'"

"Is that because of Cayce's theory that the mind can affect the body?"

"Right. Cayce's approach to health was pretty basic. In all of the readings he gave on the subject of illness, he stressed the importance of finding the root cause, not simply alleviating the symptom."

"You must get a lot of feedback on how others are helped."

Charles Thomas replied, "I'm constantly pleased at how many tell us that they feel their lives change dramatically after studying the Cayce material."

"In what way?" I asked.

"Many report that they begin to function on a higher level. Things that used to clutter their lives no longer get in the way. At this higher level of awareness there is a deeper understanding of life and its true purpose. This helps bring an inner peace." Then he added an afterthought, "They seem to find it refreshing not to be bogged down in the petty problems of everyday life."

"Shades of Shirley MacLaine," I said.

"Well Shirley MacLaine became interested in psychic development after she bought a supply of Edgar Cayce books from a California bookstore."

With those words, Charles Thomas suddenly recalled a dramatic incident. "I must tell you about a woman I met the other evening at an A.R.E. conference. We were having wine and cheese when this lady came up and introduced herself. She said that she had become involved with the A.R.E. because of a psychic experience years ago.

"She had just put her two-year-old son down for his afternoon nap," Charles Thomas began. "Then she went downstairs to do the ironing. But while she was ironing she saw an image in her mind of the little boy lying face down in water in the bathtub. She had a tremendous feeling of fear and horror. But she continued ironing, trying to put the image out of her mind because she knew with her rational mind that he was sound asleep. And besides that, he was too young to turn on the water. Each time she pushed that thought out of her mind it came back stronger and more vivid. Finally when she couldn't get rid of the fear, she put the iron down and ran upstairs. Her little boy was *not* in his bed. He was face down in the bathtub in a few inches of water. She grabbed the body, pressed the water out of his lungs, and began to give mouth-to-mouth resuscitation. Today the boy is a healthy and bright teenager. But the woman knows that her impression is what saved her son's life. She originally came to the A.R.E. because she didn't understand why she had that psychic impression.''

''You've just given me a case of goose bumps,'' I said.

''I felt the same way,'' Charles Thomas said as he buzzed his secretary. ''Marie,'' he said into an intercom on his desk, ''let's give Liz the Cook's tour.''

Within seconds Marie appeared at his office door. She was the prototype of an executive secretary, a tall brunette in a dark tailored suit who showed a pleasing aura of competence. As I said goodbye to Charles Thomas, he reminded me that we would be meeting for lunch. If I liked, he added, I could join the staff in the meditation room for their regular noon session. I told him I would like that. Then I followed Marie out into the hallway.

By the time we wound our way through the spacious gallery of the A.R.E. building, Marie had lost some of her initial reserve and told me that she had been studying the Cayce material for ten years and that it had literally changed her life. I asked her how. She hesitated for a moment, then said that she had actually been led to the A.R.E. through a dream. Dreams, according to Edgar Cayce, are to be seriously heeded. Marie explained that she was so confident that the dream was a beneficent portent that she gave up her executive secretarial job in Pennsylvania, sold her house, and moved to Virginia Beach before she even had a job lined up.

When she arrived she learned that there was a position available as secretary to the president, Charles Thomas. She applied for the position along with dozens of others. Marie told me that after she got the job she learned that Charles Thomas had taken home the applications of the best qualified people, including her own, and meditated on whom he should choose for the job.

There was a time this would have sounded quite bizarre to me. How could a dream be a direct source of wisdom and guidance? Or meditation? Could they provide really practical answers for difficult decisions? Ten years earlier, I had discovered that this was possible. My belief system changed radically as a result of my being a free-lance researcher for my husband, who was writing the strange but true story that later became known as *The Ghost of Flight 401*.

It is the story of the Eastern Airlines jet L-1011 that crashed into the Everglades in 1972. One hundred and one people died, including the flight crew. A short time later, Eastern Airlines crew members reported seeing the full-bodied apparition of the flight engineer who had been killed in the crash. He would usually appear on sister ships of the crashed L-1011 to warn of impending danger.

When John and I first began to research the flight 401 story we viewed it as simply a fascinating jet-age ghost story similar to the "Flying Dutchman." But the deeper we delved into the research, the more we realized the story was based on fact. During the course of a year's research we interviewed dozens of veteran pilots and flight attendants who claimed to have had a firsthand encounter with the ghost of the dead flight engineer. In addition, we interviewed three senior Eastern Airlines pilots who, oddly enough, were practicing psychic mediums. They had performed what is called a "soul rescue" to try to exorcise the troubled discarnate flight engineer, who was thought to be earthbound and in need of guidance to go on to his spiritual development.

In the course of this research I quite unexpectedly discovered that I had psychic ability of my own. This came about first during an experimental séance I was invited to join. I found myself revealing names, dates, and places connected to the crash of flight 401 that I had no way of consciously knowing. Later I found myself revealing factual, confirmed information about details of the deceased flight engineer's life that I could not possibly have learned by ordinary means. The result of my self-discovery was my firm conviction that psychic ability is a natural part of all of us and available to all who choose it.

But why should we choose it? That's a good question to consider before starting. Charles Thomas pointed out that the work of Edgar Cayce suggests many reasons. A primary one is to screen out the clutter of our everyday lives. Radar, searching for its distant target, can often fail because of nearby "ground clutter." This might symbolize the daily problems that constantly assault our senses.

As a mother of a small child, I can appreciate the necessity of reaching into the higher states of consciousness: A sense of peace is welcome when debating with a five-year-old why it is not sanitary to brush the dog's teeth with his toothbrush, or why eating popsicles for breakfast, lunch, and dinner will rot out his baby teeth and stunt his growth.

Fortunately Edgar Cayce recognized the vicissitudes and hardships of everyday living, and his readings offer a practical guide for achieving an inner peace that in turn will guide us toward developing our highest potential.

Cayce believed that the first job in approaching the psychic is to get rid of our ordinary conscious self and seek our higher spiritual self. If that sounds too exalted, don't let it bother you. Cayce's idea of the spiritual self can serve plenty of the needs of your physical body and your material well-being. There is no advice in any of the readings that suggests we live an ascetic lifestyle in order to develop psychic ability. Twirling a prayer wheel in the company cafeteria or chanting a mantra during an investors' meeting is not practical. Yet the Edgar Cayce readings suggest that you can literally journey through your higher consciousness twenty-four hours a day while still functioning in your daily routine. But it takes practice, plus patience and sustained application.

The benefits of your awakened latent psychic abilities are limitless. The Edgar Cayce material holds for us the high probability of much better personal health, improved emotional balance and peace, and greater capacity to think clearly and to organize our lives while we gain inner satisfaction through helping others.

As you go through the learning process, different psychic manifestations will emerge quite unexpectedly. Our intuitions will become robust and productive. Our communication with higher Spiritual Sources will provide guidance and direction to our lives. We may express great wisdom of the ages through possible contacts with these Spiritual Sources far above the ordinary plane of living.

Other manifestations that might emerge include mind-to-mind communication known as telepathy. Then there is clairvoyance, or mind-to-object communication. There is also contact between living minds and the minds of discarnate entities who are no longer living. Or there is the possibility of your own hand spontaneously beginning to write volumes of profound material without your being conscious of what your hand is writing. This is known as automatic handwriting.

Perhaps at this point you're thinking that all this sounds too much like one of those low-budget Hollywood movies that comes out around Halloween. However, Cayce made it plain that we are not to think of the paranormal as mysterious and occult, but as a very natural process that is an extension of our own conscious and unconscious minds, which reaches out beyond our ordinary five senses with proper and careful development.

Cayce is not alone in this thinking. Albert Schweitzer said, "The only road to a greater grasp of reality is the exploration of supernormal perception." The skeptical Sigmund Freud said, "If I had my life to live over again I should devote myself to psychical research rather than psychoanalysis."

A favorite quotation of mine comes from NASA scientist Robert Jastrow, who said: "For the scientist who has lived by his faith in the power of reason, the story ends like a bad dream. He has scaled the mountains of ignorance; he is about to conquer the highest peak; as he pulls himself over the final rock, he is greeted by a band of theologians who have been sitting there for centuries."

The great scientist Sir James Jeans said that the Universe looks more like a great thought than a great machine. This expresses Cayce's nonmechanistic concept of God and the Universe. From this outlook the marvels of science seem to blend with the miracles that Cayce said are available to us all.

I believe that in everyone's life there is a choice to be made that can alter his or her life radically. Robert Frost put it succinctly in his poem "A Road Not Taken."

> Two roads diverged in a yellow wood,
> And sorry I could not travel both
>
> I took the one less traveled by,
> And that has made all the difference.

When I approached the fork in the road I faced a choice: I could head down a smooth superhighway bound by my five senses with no exit ramps to see what lay beyond. Or I could take the road less traveled and discover the larger reality that supersedes the senses. I'm glad I chose the latter—a path that winds through the lush landscape of the higher consciousness, revealing new vistas at every turn.

As Marie led me toward the Cayce library, I thought about the "road less traveled," the road that led me to Edgar Cayce. I stepped into the orderly library filled with endless volumes and archival records of Edgar Cayce and books on related subjects. As I did, I had the distinct feeling that the more than fourteen thousand psychic readings bound in large leather binders rimming the walls held the key to questions that could profoundly affect our lives.

1

RELEASING THE SELF

Reaching Toward the Source

With our feet planted solidly on Cayce's foundation we can
begin to seek an altered state of consciousness through
guided meditation. The object is to open the self to the
bright light of the original Creative Source that put us here
into our consciousness. We are dipping into the Infinite
Intelligence of the Universe where all knowledge and wisdom reside.

Edgar Cayce believed that if we were properly instructed,
we could all project our unconscious minds into this great
omniscient reservoir. Often I try to picture Edgar Cayce
lying on his battered studio couch, eyes closed, in deep
trance, dictating to his wife or secretary in a soft articulate
voice, his mind and soul immersed in the canopy of the
Universe, churning out indisputable wisdom. It seems as if
he might have been lying on his back in a planetarium with
a complete celestial encyclopedia projected on its concave
dome with infinite words scrolling across it.

Any rational mind is bound to be puzzled by the miracles
that Cayce performed. Yet the clues I have found in science

19

demonstrate that his work is not as far beyond reason as it appears at first glance.

Science Meets the Psychic

There is little argument that everything in the physical world consists of energy, from the atom and its particles on up. There is also little argument that energy is everywhere. It is inexhaustible and timeless. Since anything that appears to be solid is simply a concentration of energy, the barrier between the spiritual and the material is not as formidable as it may seem. We are all bathed in this limitless force of energy and it is reasonable to believe that we can make contact with it and draw on its inexhaustible power if we open ourselves fully to it.

Three of the world's greatest inventors, Thomas A. Edison, Guglielmo Marconi, and Nikola Tesla all believed the same thing. They stated that some day it would be possible to invent a device to converse with the dead. In fact, in 1920, *Scientific American* published an interview with Edison. He was quoted as saying: "I have been thinking for some time of a machine or apparatus which could be operated by personalities who have passed on to another existence or sphere." Later in the interview, he added that he hoped to be able to complete the machine "before many months." He never did complete it, although recent experiments in Europe and the United States are showing persuasive evidence of such a development.

Like these great inventors, Cayce believed that communication with other levels of existence was a distinct reality. But before we reach the point where this is possible we must elevate our awareness to become attuned to the Spiritual Forces beyond the five senses.

The Altered State of Mind

The details of how to reach your own altered state of consciousness through meditation will follow, but the objective must be kept in mind. We need to empty ourselves of the distractions of the physical senses.

One seeker of psychic ability wrote to Cayce to ask if in his physical body he would ever be able to see and hear on a higher plane. Cayce pointed out several fundamental concepts. One was that the body of any individual consists of more than one consciousness, each on a different plane: the spiritual, the mental, and the physical. He added that as we open ourselves to spheres beyond our five senses we will experience new insights in hearing and feeling. This is accomplished, he told us, in only one way: through meditation.

"It [meditation] is not musing, not daydreaming; but as ye find your bodies made of the physical, mental, and spiritual, it is attuning of the mental body and the physical body to its spiritual source," Cayce said (281–41). Once we make this attunement, he told us, all knowledge and wisdom will be available to us.

Preparing for Meditation

Before meditation, our spiritual and mental preparation is vital. Cayce emphasized getting rid of our hostilities and resentments. He said that hate, malice, and jealousy only create poisons with the minds, souls, and bodies of people. In another reading Cayce said: that anger can destroy the brain as well as any disease. The readings make clear that wiping out negativity is one of the most important things

we have to do in order to open ourselves up as clear channels
for psychic development.

Removing Ancient Grudges

I can name a few people in public or private life who bring
out my primitive instincts at the flash of a thought. I can
even get a perverse high from dwelling on things that others
have said or done to irk me. Some of the things I find myself
dredging up border on the ludicrous. In fact, the other day
my blood curdled as I recalled my brother ripping the tail
off my Davy Crockett hat when I was six years old. I stopped
myself before I manufactured a whole scenario about how
that incident affected my entire life. John once confessed
that he still gets worked up over the time his sister bopped
him on the head with a cast-iron spoon.

I'm constantly reminding myself how every negative
thought that flashes across my mind leaves a scar. To get
rid of the negative thinking, I try to picture hitting the erase
key on my typewriter to wipe out the thought. It's not always
easy to follow Cayce's advice, but it is rewarding: He told
us that we must manifest gentleness, kindness, and patience.
Cayce believed that these were the beauties of life and the
more these qualities were exhibited the more they would
bloom.

" . . . if one would correct physical or mental disturbances," Cayce said, "it is necessary to change the attitude
and to let the life forces become constructive and not de-
structive" (3312–1).

There's no question that when your thoughts stray to the
negative you're wasting time and energy on a nonproductive
enterprise. The waste of time is damaging enough. But
medical researchers are now finding that a negative person

is more likely to suffer from cancer, heart disease, high blood pressure, and strokes.

At the opposite end of the spectrum, researchers are discovering that positive personalities are linked to enhanced physical and emotional health. On February 3, 1987, the *New York Times* ran an article that affirmed the power of positive thinking. It stated that research confirms that pessimism is linked to problems of shyness and depression. Pollyanna was right, the article said. Optimism can pay dividends of health, longer life, job success, and higher scores on I.Q. tests.

Cayce was fifty years ahead of his time in this kind of thinking. He claimed that no one can hate his neighbor and escape stomach or liver trouble. Nor could anyone indulge in jealous anger and not end up with upset digestion or a heart condition.

In studying the Cayce material I soon learned that he had a flair for salting his readings with humor to drive home a point. One man asked if there was a probability of bad health in March. Cayce responded that if he was looking for bad health, he could have it in February. If he wanted to skip March, he could have it in June. And if he wanted to skip June, he didn't have to have it at all!

This witty response seems to sum up that our state of mind is directly linked to our physical body. The way we respond to life's situations plays a major role in instigating or worsening an illness. However, a therapy that is designed to bring the body, mind, and soul into attunement will result in health. Cayce said that we should tune ourselves as we would tune a violin for harmony. He believed that when our body and soul are attuned to the Infinite, we will become more sensitive, allowing for spiritual and material things to be better enjoyed.

Love Yourself First

Love, according to Cayce, is the central motivating force that stimulates psychic ability. He believed that the first lesson we must learn about love is that love begins by loving yourself in an unselfish way. But before you can love yourself you have to forgive yourself. Cayce said we must keep ourselves from condemning others, and, equally important, we must not condemn ourselves. In other words, don't keep punishing yourself for past offenses. Instead he told us: "Look for the good and ye will find it. Search for it, for it is a pearl of great price" (1776–1).

Once you have found the "pearl" in yourself, it is easy to recognize it in others. Cayce was once asked by a woman why she was so often disappointed in friends who turned out to be selfish and self-centered. She wanted to know if she was too intolerant and lacked understanding.

Cayce didn't mince words. He asked the woman if she was not seeing her own reflection. Instead of finding fault, he believed that we should cultivate affection. If we want to have friends, we should be friendly. If we want to have love, we should be loving. Cayce said that these were natural laws that apply in spiritual things and in personal relationships.

Love Is the Key

Throughout the readings Cayce suggested that love is the key to unlocking the door to our higher consciousness so we may tap into the Creative Force. He said that it is the "Love Intent" that fosters psychic perception within us.

This is why parents and children, husbands and wives, siblings, and close friends so often report instances of extrasensory perception, especially in times of need. One friend, a card-carrying skeptic, told me about the time he woke up in the middle of the night in a cold sweat. He had dreamed that the braces on his daughter's teeth were locked together. He woke up his wife to tell her of the dream. The next morning his daughter came down to the breakfast table and said that in the middle of the night she had awakened with her braces stuck together and had panicked. The friend claimed that this incident caused him to reconsider his hard-nosed view of reality.

Another graphic example of how the "Love Intent" promotes psychic ability happened to me not long ago. John and I drove out to a luncheon with two of our very close friends. All the way home the couple was very depressed. The husband was an actor who had been out of work for many months. The bills were piling up. They were desperate. I could actually feel their grief as if it were my own. I went into a brief meditative state and asked to be given some sort of inner advice that could help my friends over their hurdle.

As we pulled into their driveway I suddenly blurted out that our actor friend must phone his agent immediately. I told him that I had just received a strong flash that there was a major role for him on a television show. As he got out of the car he said, "Liz, you're just fantasizing the impossible!" Just before he opened the front door I heard the phone ringing inside. It was his agent. The agent asked him to come to his office the following day to audition for a major role in *As the World Turns*. He got the part.

And still another incident happened in my life to point out how a strong emotional bond of love can bring forth psychic ability. This time I had been pulling out of our driveway in our small Toyota. Suddenly I heard John yell my name. It was so loud and clear that it sounded as if he were in the car with me. I slammed on my brakes and turned to see a huge truck speed by. If I had not slammed on the brakes at that very moment, my car and I would have become a tangle of Japanese modern art.

Trembling, I went back into the house fully prepared for John to lecture for twenty minutes on what a lousy driver I was. Instead he was calmly reading the newspaper. I thanked him for saving my life. He didn't know what I was talking about. I explained how I had heard his voice, slammed on the brakes, and averted the passing truck. John thought for a moment and said that a few minutes earlier he had heard a large truck speed by the house. As it did, he had a strange flutter and said to himself, "I hope Liz is cautious when she pulls out of the driveway."

Fear: A Dead-Bolt Lock

If love is the key to unlocking the doors to our higher consciousness, then fear is a dead-bolt lock. Cayce told us that fear is a major block to releasing our psychic nature and to everything else constructive in life. We can get rid of fear by making ourselves One with the Universe and with the One Creative Force that permeates and supersedes everything. This may sound a bit abstract. A crude comparison might be that if you were caught in an undertow, you could struggle fiercely against it, exhaust yourself, and drown. If you had known that the undertow was pulling you toward a safe, dry sandbar, you could have floated with the tide to be deposited safe and dry.

Lesson of the Oneness

Cayce pictured the great Constructive Forces of the Universe as pulling us toward a safe, dry sandbar and suggested that we release our fears. Or to borrow the vernacular, go with the flow. Cayce believed that the lesson of the Oneness of all force lies within each person—materially, mentally, morally, and spiritually. In that Oneness, fear and doubt will be automatically cast aside.

Getting Rid of Fear

In reading 2540–1 I came across a prayer Cayce suggested for us to use to get rid of fear. It reads: "When fear of the future occurs, or fear of the past, or fear of what others will say—put all such away with this prayer—not merely by mouth, not merely by thoughts, but in body, in mind and in soul say: HERE I AM LORD—THINE! KEEP ME IN THE WAY THOU WOULD HAVE ME GO, RATHER THAN IN THAT I MIGHT CHOOSE."

Cayce was urging us to walk in the light of the Creative Forces, and if we do, we will not be afraid. We must turn our backs to material circumstances. Since Cayce considered fear to be one of the greatest foes of the physical body, he advised us to take every step to remove it to avoid severe problems with circulation, liver, spleen, lymphatic system, and digestion.

Many people who have been in a life-or-death situation actually claim to be "fear-free" due to a deeply religious experience. Fifteen years ago I had a close brush with death. The experience altered my perception of life. It happened

while I was a flight attendant for Northwest Orient Airlines.
We were four hours out of Honolulu on our way to Tokyo.
Nearly five more hours stretched ahead of us when the senior
flight attendant whispered to me to show no alarm; she said
that within an hour we would most likely have to ditch into
the Pacific. Then she told me to grab my flight manual and
proceed to the cockpit for further briefing.

Once I was inside the 747 cockpit, the captain explained
the situation. "We have a problem getting the fuel from the
inboard main tanks. We think the tank valve is locked in
transit. If that's the case, we won't have enough fuel to get
to Tokyo or back to Honolulu."

After a quick briefing that covered the eight evacuation
doors and exits, emergency equipment, passenger and main
cabin preparation, ditching stations, and finally abandoning
the aircraft, he sent us back to our posts to await further
instructions.

I sat down in my assigned jumpseat numb with fear. My
mind flashed back to the time I was hired by the airline.
The interviewer asked me point-blank how I felt about the
possibility of being in a crash. I answered exactly how I
thought he'd like to be answered: "I've never minded
dying." I realized immediately how silly my answer was.
He looked at me as if I were demented. I certainly couldn't
tell him the truth and expect to get the job. The truth of the
matter was that no two words in the English language struck
as much terror in my bones as death and dying.

I flipped open the manual and turned to the section on
"Survival at Sea." Suddenly the captain rang a succession
of chimes, indicating that ditching was inevitable.

I got up from my seat. My knees were banging together.
The captain announced over the P.A. that we would be
evacuating the plane. I began to offer comfort to passengers
who were as scared as I. For a few moments after the

announcement the cabin was eerily silent. Then one person had an emotional outburst and others followed.

A little boy traveling with his mother grabbed onto my leg. He was crying for his father, whom they were on their way to see. I tried to distract him by asking him to help me pass out pillows and blankets. A couple on their honeymoon were locked together, sobbing. An elderly lady had her arms around a young soldier who was holding his fiancée's photo. He was calling her name loudly into the night. A mother began to nurse her infant. Her face was pasted against the tiny head. A businessman sat motionless, staring vacantly at a family photo in his wallet.

Moments later more chimes sounded, indicating it was time to put on the uninflated life vests and get into the ditching position, head rested on knees, arms wrapped around legs. As the plane began its descent I suddenly realized that I was no longer afraid. It was as if I had lost my own ego. I would have gladly given up my life for that little boy and his father, or for the young couple on their honeymoon, or for the soldier and his fiancée, or for the mother and her infant. I was actually willing to die for people I didn't even know. I felt as if I were part of them. We were one. I had transcended my physical body and merged with a much greater reality. The only thing that was real was love for my fellow human beings.

Suddenly the plane leveled off. At first I thought I had only imagined it. Then somebody shouted, ''Hey, we're not descending anymore.'' The captain came over the P.A., his voice soft and strained. I could detect a distinct quiver. ''Folks,'' he said, ''the good Lord is with us this evening. At less than five thousand feet above sea level our transit valve miraculously unlocked. We're getting fuel fast and furious. See you all on the ground in Tokyo.''

Whenever I feel fear rear its ugly head, I reflect on that

incident. I also reflect on what Cayce said: "Fear is that element in the character and in the experience of individuals which brings about more of trouble than any other influence in the experience of an entity. For, when ye are sure of the right path and follow it, ye do not fear" (2560–1).

More Stumbling Blocks

In addition to negative emotions, such as fear, anger, hostility, and resentment, strong desires can also be considered stumbling blocks that prevent us from opening ourselves to the meditative process. At times we all cling unnecessarily to people and objects, believing that our happiness will come from sources outside ourselves. It is this thinking that usually sets us up for frustration and disappointment. How many times have you finally achieved your goal and felt an emptiness inside?

Cayce explained this feeling of emptiness as a warning signal that our physical and spiritual natures are out of balance. He believed that our first step toward psychic development is to acknowledge that we are both spiritual and physical beings. Both sides must be nourished.

To expand our higher senses we must "let go" of all strong physical and emotional desires. These desires make us unable to see the greater picture of ourselves. By focusing on our narrow desires, we are shutting out other possibilities.

Realize that by letting go you are releasing yourself from the burden of carrying these heavy desires around. Once you let them go, you will be free to explore your greater self. You are about to alter your perception not of only yourself but of the world around you. In turn you will gain a richer understanding on a higher, more constructive level, which will make it easier for you to achieve your goals.

Letting Go Exercise

How about an exercise to practice how to get rid of the heavy desires that often block you from the feeling of self-freedom? As usual with this sort of exercise, it's best to lie back, clear your mind, and make yourself comfortable. Now you are free to let your mind create a few images as if they were projected on a movie screen inside your mind.

First conjure up the image of a vast expanse of the starlit sky with the planets, galaxies, and countless stars all tumbling around one another in harmonious rhythm and beautifully synchronized motion. All are moving smoothly under the guidance of a magnificent Creative Force that has everything under control. Imagine yourself as part of this. Realize that this is the Oneness that welds everything together including your own life and destiny. In the face of this magnificent and awesome display, picture your own desires. Perhaps it's a desire for a relationship, a promotion, a vacation, a house, a new job, or anything else. Now make an image of these desires and drop them into your open hands. Then squeeze those images tightly in your fists and hold on with white knuckles. Open your hands suddenly. Let the desires escape into thin air. Just like a trekker dropping off a heavy knapsack, you'll feel lighter and relieved of a burden.

Remember, you're not going to throw that knapsack away. You're simply giving yourself a rest. Now feel yourself lighter and lighter and free of a burden. Be confident that by releasing yourself in this way you can find a different way to achieve what you want within the celestial harmony of the Universe. Your desires may be only burdens because strong desires often are stumbling blocks rather than steppingstones. Buddha found that the main cause of discontent for everyone was simply Desire. Letting go of it can bring deep satisfaction and fulfillment in a different way than you had imagined.

Warmup to Meditation: Visualization

Before getting into the formal steps of meditation, let's try another visualization. Simply make yourself comfortable by lying back or relaxing in a chair and closing your eyes. Remember that your goal is to get rid of all distractions so you may surrender yourself to the Creative Forces and to make yourself part of them. Now picture yourself bathed in the Infinite Energy of the Universe. Imagine yourself fully part of it, floating in it. After all, everything that exists is energy, whether it's in the form of light or warmth. God is considered by many as pure light and love. Cayce considered us to be fully immersed in the Mind of God.

Forget about the solidity of matter for a while. For instance, an ice cube feels very solid indeed. Drop it in boiling water and you can see how solid it remains. Picture God's energy as a cloud of pure and Divine steam coming toward you. Then picture your not-so-solid body as a cloud of equally Divine steam, for after all, you are part of God. Now imagine your own cloud of steam merging with that of the Creator, blending easily with it as the two vapors meet and merge effortlessly.

You are now part of God. His energy has filled you and you can begin to draw on this Infinite Creative Energy. It is yours to use toward your own best constructive goals. Here you are now, with every cell of your body filled with this Divine inflow. So relax and enjoy it and ask to put it to the best constructive use.

Review

Let's review what we've learned from Edgar Cayce so far. First, there's the reason for wanting to develop our psychic ability. We want to rip the cobwebs away from our everyday routine so that we may reach into our higher consciousness for a richer understanding of the purpose of our lives. We're all being swept along in a relentless river of time. We can't swim against it so we might as well join it. We can steer around the obstacles in it through our own will, confident that the current is going to take us to the right place. Our psychic senses can give us the right instinct for a safe voyage. But Cayce told us that before our psychic senses can go to work for us, we must first rid ourselves of all the distractions that stand in our way. Fear, anger, hostility, and strong desires are blocks that prevent us from rising to a state of Cosmic Consciousness. Love, Cayce said, is a direct pipeline to our higher selves. In this state our full potential may be realized.

We've learned that matter and the spiritual are not so far apart since matter is energy, as the latest developments in physics confirm. And we've also experimented with two visualizations to help balance our physical and spiritual natures, paving the way for the next step in our psychic development—meditation.

2

MEDITATION: MASTER KEY TO THE THE PSYCHIC

Meditation Defined

Now you are ready to extend your program of development. You must move slowly and take it step by step. Patience and persistence are important. Cayce told us, "Meditation is listening to the Divine within" (1861–9). It is setting aside a specific time each day to shut out the distractions of everyday life so that we may enter within for spiritual, physical, and mental nourishment. We are reminded that in prayer we speak to God. But in meditation God speaks to us.

With this in mind, our meditations will become a journey inward to discover a deeper awareness of life and a greater degree of inner peace.

Setting an Ideal

Cayce believed that meditation must always be accompanied by an ideal or a goal. First, he said, we must find our ideal,

35

and then enter meditation with a worthy purpose. The ideal should not be merely vocal. We should write our ideal down under these three headings: Spiritual, Mental, and Material. We may find that our ideals change from time to time on the premise that each soul grows in grace, knowledge, and understanding.

Cayce was once asked what the best method was to reach the divine power or psychic force within and draw on it for knowledge, strength, power, and direction.

He responded that this ability lies latent within. First we must find deep within ourselves the ideal to reach for. We should know that the Creator has promised to meet us within. As we turn within, we should meditate on that premise so that we become conscious of that At-Oneness with our Creator. This will bring us guidance to achieve what we are seeking.

Physical Benefits of Meditation

I first took up meditation fifteen years ago. My father wanted to know if I was going to shave my head, wear a white robe, and hand out flowers at Cleveland Hopkins Airport. Back then many people lumped meditation with the pet rock and moondust. Within a half-dozen years, however, meditation was being taken more seriously. Studies began to reveal that regular meditators had fewer absences from work due to illness. Furthermore, they seemed to exhibit a stronger sense of well-being. These health rewards prompted the largest corporations in the country to offer meditation seminars to their employees.

Cayce had heralded the health benefits of meditation thirty years earlier. He said that individuals who draw on the Creative Forces deep within themselves may alter their surroundings and the vibrations of their bodies. He believed that all healing forces are within, not without. Healing, according to Cayce, is attuning each atom of the body to the awareness of the Divine that lies within each cell.

Simply, Cayce believed that through meditation we may direct Divine Energy to influence material manifestations. Medical science is now telling us the same thing, although not calling it "Divine Energy." Researchers have concluded that our mental attitude has a direct bearing on our immune system. This reminds me of Cayce's belief that what we think, we become.

Nothing Mysterious

Meditation is simple, but not easy. It requires discipline. To be effective it should be done every day at a regular time and place for fifteen or twenty minutes just as if you were keeping office hours with yourself. Your objective should be to seek an altered state of consciousness. This condition must be thought of as a light trance, a hazy state of being half asleep, half awake in which your immediate surroundings seem to fade into the background. There is nothing mysterious about it.

After sitting comfortably away from distractions, the instruction is simple: Be still! This simple step can often be difficult. Silence is hard to come by. I know that in my own case, I meditate in the morning after I have dropped off my son at preschool and the noise levels have once again returned to normal.

Cayce's steps in reaching the altered state roughly follow the traditions of yoga but are simpler and less stringent. Some mild exercises are considered helpful as you prepare to meditate.

Cayce's Head Roll Exercise

One exercise recommended by Cayce is a form of a head roll. It's gentle and easy. First you sit erect with your spine straight. Then you drop your head forward until your chin rests on your chest. Then you bring your head upright to its natural position, and slowly perform this three times.

Next, you drop your head back and bring it upright three times. Now tilt your head to the left, bringing your ear close to your shoulder, then bring your head upright, and perform this three times. After you tilt your head to the right three times, begin a slow roll counterclockwise by dropping your chin to your chest and rolling your head completely around until your chin returns to your chest. Then roll clockwise to the right in the same way. Perform the left and right head roll three times.

Cayce referred to this routine as a warmup for meditation. He advised that we not hurry ourselves or become anxious about the process. We should clear our conscious mind and enter our "inner temple," which he calls the human body. The object that should be kept in mind is to lose our awareness of the physical body as much as possible.

Awakening Our Spiritual Centers

Although we may make ourselves comfortable lying on our back in bed or on the floor, we have other options, such as sitting in a chair. In either of these positions, Cayce regarded it as important that we keep our spine straight. This allows a free flow of our Creative Energies. Cayce believed there are seven spiritual centers in the body that are awakened through meditation. These spiritual centers have been rec-

ognized since the earliest days of Eastern thought. They are
located in the ductless glands whose functions still are a bit
of a medical puzzle. With all the intrusions of the modern
materialistic world, Cayce felt, the gland system had lapsed
into desuetude. Meditation may bring it back into constructive spiritual use and enhance our physical, spiritual, and
mental capacities.

It is through these spiritual centers that Cayce, along with
the ancients, felt that the basic Life Force surges. A straight
spine, we learn, provides a superhighway for this Creative
Force so that it can flow through everything.

Focusing the Mind by Using an Affirmation

Once you have quieted your body, you'll have to quiet your
mind. That's the hard part. Cayce suggested the use of
affirmations to keep your mind focused and to help separate
you from the physical. He also believed that repeating an
affirmation will set the spiritual vibrations in motion.

A few of Edgar Cayce's favorite affirmations are:

*"Do that thou KNOWEST to do TODAY, and then
the next step may be given thee"* (2300–1).

*"For to hold grudges, to hold malice, to hold those
things that create or bring contention, only builds the
barrier to prevent thy OWN inner self enjoying peace
and contentment"* (361–16).

*"Know thyself, then, to be as a corpuscle, as a facet,
as a characteristic, as a love, in the body of God"*
(2533–7).

Cayce acknowledged that everybody's affirmations will be different because everyone has different needs and desires. In addition to the use of affirmations, Cayce recognized the value of chants and mantras of yoga practice in tuning our vibrations to higher levels. Everything in existence is based on vibrations. Music, so important to the soul, consists of nothing but vibrations. So it is with our bodies, minds, and souls.

The Way to Breathe

Deep breathing is a foundation of meditation. Cayce felt that such breathing opens the spiritual centers and that the life force is propelled through the centers to release the physical consciousness and turn it over to the Universal Force.

Close the left nostril with your finger. Breathe deeply through the right nostril and hold the breath for a moment, then close the right nostril with your finger and exhale slowly through the left nostril. Repeat this three times. Now reverse the process by breathing three times through the left nostril and exhaling through the right.

As you inhale, picture that you are pulling strength into your body system. Do each exercise at least three times. But you may continue for as long as you feel the process is helping you lose your self-awareness. Some might repeat this for ten or fifteen minutes.

American Health (November 1986) reported on the possible benefits to the brain of exercises that balance breathing through the left and right nostrils as described in some yoga disciplines and in the Edgar Cayce readings.

While breathing, you may let your eyes close or simply stare vacantly into the distance. You may want to have quiet and relaxing music in the background. I like to meditate to soft Celtic harp music.

As you continue to breathe, you should still keep in mind that you are striving for one major goal: to join forces with the Universe, to harmonize with it completely, to put yourself at its disposal, to let your own will go and be part of the Universe as you strip away all your past worries, resentments, and frustrations.

You may be asking yourself: How will I know when I have reached the freedom of my altered state? When this happens, you may actually feel yourself lifting above and away from your immediate surroundings. They seem to drop out of existence even though you are partially aware of them, as you feel yourself rising higher and higher.

Raising Vibrations by Chanting a Mantra

To reach an optimal psychic state we may try to raise our vibrations toward a higher spiritual plane, perhaps raise them to vibrate in unison with God's own infinite vibrations. To experiment with this device it is worth trying some of the yoga mantras that have been practiced for centuries. The classic Buddhist mantra, Om Mani Padme Aum, has a resonance that can be felt within the brain and body as we prolong the last syllable, keeping the thought that we are part of the great Universal plan as we do so.

Another mantra is simply holding the sounds of "I ammmm," resonating for as long as we feel the vibrations. Buddhists have a saying of great simple beauty: "Every sound you hear is mantra. Everyone you see is a Buddha. Everything you see is Nirvana." Thinking this while you repeat a mantra can contribute to your inner peace and help you express the universal love that Cayce found most important for all of us, and especially important as we open ourselves as psychic channels.

Edgar Cayce had been asked many questions about experiencing vibrations while in a meditative state. In one reading a man said that his entire body seemed to be vibrating to the thought that he had opened his ear to the unseen forces that surround the throne of grace, beauty, and might.

Cayce replied that these experiences should remain sacred, that the meditator can expect more of the same. The readings, however, caution us against expecting any particular experience, because we may limit the ways in which the Divine may manifest to us. Cayce stated, "Oft we find individual activity becomes so personal in even the meditation that there is sought this or that [special desire] which may have been reported to have happened to another. . . . And in this manner there is cut away, there is built the barrier which prevents the real inner self from *experiencing*" (705–2).

The first time I experienced what Cayce referred to as "vibrations of a spiritual nature" was during a meditation with Buddhist monks of the remote Tengboche Monastery on a high peak in the Himalayas. I could actually feel my spiritual self lift to the point where I felt connected to a Cosmic Consciousness, creating a resonance of peace and tranquility that I had never experienced before.

Perhaps this was induced by the contemplative atmosphere of the monastery, which was such a marked contrast to Western life. Here the High Lama told me that most Buddhists feel that Westerners have underdeveloped spiritual lives and a grossly material focus.

The people of the high Himalayas seemed to be paying for their joy and zest and love for their fellow being by material deprivation. In the West, however, we were paying for our material comforts by spiritual deprivation. The question is: Which group is living a greater illusion? As the philosopher Tsong-kha-pa wrote: ''All worldly things are brief, like lightning in the sky. This life you must know as a tiny splash of a raindrop; a thing of beauty that disappears even as it comes into being.''

Intensifying the Altered State

You may want to experiment with a lighted candle as a device for intensifying the altered state. Staring at and concentrating on the flame during meditation can help screen out the distractions of our physical mind and body and permit the deep unconscious mind, which Cayce considered the seat of the soul, to come to the surface. Suspending our ordinary mental perceptions is important because we are trying to rid ourselves of the physical and mental planes so that we permit the Spiritual Sources to come through us as we serve as a dedicated channel.

To use a candle effectively, you must keep your eyes rigidly on the flame, forcing them back if they should wander away from the flame even momentarily. Eye fatigue may set in, but this is part of the discipline. You may notice that your surroundings seem to fade out of existence, but again this is part of the process of freeing yourself from your ordinary senses and surroundings. You may feel a floating sensation and relaxation of the body. Again, this is desirable. Merely staring in this way at a spot on the wall may produce a similar experience.

At the same time you might visualize emptying yourself of the day's plans and distractions, draining them out and opening yourself to that Divine inflow. Picture it rinsing and nourishing every cell in your body as you tune into the One Source that created those cells and everything else. By visualizing yourself in total harmony with the Universe, you can try to look into the Universal Mind as Cayce did.

Remember that we are trying to seek a higher purpose in everything we do. As we stare at a flame with our minds open, images and flashes of thoughts might go through our minds. Pay attention to them. They may emanate from the sources beyond ourselves and provide us with valuable intuition, which is an integral part of the psychic.

The Importance of Intuition

You may now find you are fit to let your intuition go to work at its highest capacity. Cayce told us that intuition plays a major part in psychic development and is an integral part of it. Our deepest intuitive forces go beyond our cramped mental thinking, which is limited to the material world only. The psychic goes beyond the mental, although it does not replace it. Cayce said that if we are attuned to the higher Spiritual Forces, then our hunches should always be followed. If they are of a constructive nature and balanced with judgment, love, and decisive action, we must listen to our inner voice and our strong gut feelings at all times.

Cayce suggested that our first impressions are often more sound than those reached after long contemplation. He believed that confusion arises when the advice of others differs from our voice within. Cayce went on to say that this inner voice is the true expression of our soul, which endures through infinity.

Maybe you're wondering how you can be sure of your gut feeling. What if you're wrong? Not long ago my husband, John, was confused. A major magazine phoned him with an assignment in a war-torn zone. Immediately John turned the story down. However, a short time later he had second thoughts. Friends began telling John that it was a perfect story for him. John was torn. His Indiana Jones macho persona was telling him to pack his bags. On the other hand, his Woody Allen, card-carrying hypochondriac self was telling him to shred his passport.

Before John took any drastic steps, I gave him a test that I had read about in a British journal for psychical research. The simple test was a way to measure the validity of your intuitive experience. I told John to sit back in a chair and ask himself: Am I supposed to do the story? If he suddenly felt his entire body lifting forward, he should go. However, if he felt his body pasted to the back of the chair, as if some sort of celestial glue was preventing him from packing his bags, he should not go. The latter happened. The story turned out to be a dud, reinforcing Cayce's theory that our first impressions are more sound than those arrived after long contemplation. Cayce, however, believed that we should not act on these first impressions until after meditation. "On any question that arises, ask the mental self— get the answer, yes or no. Rest on that. Do not act immediately (if you would develop the intuitive influences). Then, in meditation or prayer, when looking within self, ask—is this yes or no? The answer is intuitive development" (282–4).

Developing Intuition

According to Cayce, intuition is something that we should view as quite a natural occurrence. "[Intuition] is the innate expressions of the inner self" (276–6).

Cayce recommended four specific methods for developing

our intuition. The first is through meditation. "Intuitive forces are developed more by the introspective activities" (282–3). Meditation is the most direct way to attune ourselves to the Spiritual Forces within. Cayce also said that during and shortly after meditation are the times we are most receptive to intuitive insights.

The second method for developing our intuition is simply to trust our inner selves. By this, Cayce meant that we should begin with small decisions and gradually trust our inner voice as much as our analytical mind. He tells us: "The more and more each is impelled by that which is intuitive, or the relying upon the soul force within, the greater, the farther, the deeper, the broader, the more constructive may be the result" (792–2).

The third method is to pay close attention to impressions that come just as we are falling asleep and just as we awaken. Intuitive impressions, Cayce said, are easily "caught" at these times.

The fourth and last method is to make every effort to develop our creative imagination. "For anyone with great imagination, of course, is intuitive," Cayce said (744–1). He was referring to the fact that people who express their creativity, whether through painting, dancing, baking, writing, gardening, or photography, are naturally exercising their imaginations. While in this creative frame of mind, the analytical nature is relaxed, allowing the intuitive flow to surface.

An Experiment with Friends: Releasing Upward to the Infinite

You've absorbed enough of Cayce's basic ideas about drawing out your latent psychic talents to go through some of the mechanics that might help you bring them out. As an experiment, let's pretend that you and I are seated opposite each other. Seat yourself as comfortably as you can with a straight spine and plant your feet firmly on the floor. You might, if you wish, place your hands on your knees and lean slightly forward. Cayce believed strongly in group meditation, so you might try a session with one or more friends. Your spiritual growth and mine is enhanced by others. Mutual support can often grow in a common brotherhood.

Now let's begin our breathing exercises, fully ready to release ourselves to the highest Spiritual Forces. Breathe in slowly and deeply through the nose and hold your breath for a few moments. Imagine that you are breathing in strength and love, which are filling your mind and body. Let them fill you so that there's no room for anything else. Now exhale slowly through your lips. As you do, visualize that you are expelling all hostilities and resentments.

Let's begin again with a deep breath. Can you feel and imagine strength and light of the highest Spiritual Forces coursing through you? Picture them flooding every cell in your body, draining away all the negative. Again, hold your breath for a few moments and slowly exhale. Can you picture the detritus of negative thoughts being expelled with your breath? Have you breathed in all the positive and unlimited power of the Creative Universe? Feel its power reside in you, for it is limitless. Now repeat the process slowly, breathing in and out, out and in, fully in harmony and in unison with the Universe.

Let's do this over and over for five minutes or so, each time picturing that we are releasing ourselves to the highest spiritual power beyond ourselves. Let's feel ourselves more and more relaxed and our problems of the day dropping away and out of sight. Continue the breathing in unison with me, and both of us might picture our vibrations in unison with the vibrations of the highest spiritual order.

Picture a scene of serenity and tranquility as we draw ourselves away from a turbulent world to join a realm where a perfect consciousness resides, far over and above the finite. Forget the clamor. You are providing your soul with a passport and visa to a spiritually verdant land. It's guaranteed clamor-free if you will let yourself go there. Now as you continue your breathing, close your eyes if you wish. We're aware of each other's presence. We're both immersed in a sphere far above our petty and limited five senses.

As we breathe more let's feel our bodies growing lighter and lighter so that we are beginning to lift from our chairs. Now picture yourself lifting slowly higher, moving upward and upward until you feel free, and even soaring away from the confines of the earth. In your mind's eye you can picture yourself looking down on earth.

Now that we're both soaring high above the earth, let's turn ourselves to our purpose: We're ready to join with the highest Spiritual Source. We're letting ourselves become part of this limitless energy and intelligence. We can now tap into it as long as our motives are constructive. Let's allow ourselves to feel the repose of the Infinite. Let it soothe our minds and our bodies in its perfection.

Why don't we try applying some of the things we're learning on our journey? Maybe we'd like to give some thought to the coming day. We can ask for some constructive help about what we want to accomplish today. Remember our purpose is blending and tuning into the harmony of the Creative Force so that we can apply it for the good of ourselves and others. With that in mind, we might turn to some important decisions we have to make during the day. Let's be still in our meditation and listen. Listen to that inner voice within each of us.

All through this process we may get valuable help. If we

don't have immediate results, there's nothing to worry about because practice and patience are important. We may, however, reach the state at which we are ready to try several small experiments that will foreshadow the possibilities for further psychic developments.

3

PUTTING THE PSYCHIC TO WORK

Reaching Beyond the Five Senses

At this point it would be worthwhile to examine the mechanics of how your psychic ability might emerge. We'll take a look at three of the basic activities that reach beyond the five senses, often with very surprising results even for the beginner.

The first of these activities is called psychometry. This is the technique of holding a personal object of your experimental subject, such as a ring, watch, or bracelet, and suspending your conscious mind so that spontaneous images can reveal facts about the subject that you would have no way of knowing with your conscious mind.

The second psychic activity we will experiment with is telepathy. This is the transference of information from mind to mind. It is not to be confused with clairvoyance, which is the discernment of objects or events without the involvement of another person's mind.

The third psychic activity is called remote viewing. Remote viewing is the process of projecting the unconscious mind to a distant location where your unconscious mind sees events exactly as they are happening. It involves both telepathy and clairvoyance, and is quite a common experience in psychic practice.

A psychic reading can be given using any of these three tools. For many people the mention of a psychic reading may conjure up the image of the effusive medium, Madame Arcarti, in Noel Coward's play *Blythe Spirit*. I remember the first psychic reading I had. I was in my early twenties living in Minneapolis. The only reason I went was because my roommates had given me the reading as a birthday gift. The psychic, who did look a little like Madame Arcarti, told me several things that I have never forgotten. She said that I would move east. Five years later I did, in spite of the fact that I always wanted to live in the West. She told me that I would marry a man much older than myself, which I did. John refers to himself as a teenage geriatric. And she told me that I was going to be rich. She was right on that score, too. I am rich. But not in dollars. En route to developing my higher self, my earthly cravings seem to have become anesthetized.

As a kid I couldn't wait to get out of Cleveland Heights, move to Hollywood, and break into the movies where I would be flooded in money, jewels, Cadillacs, and gaudy homes. Had I had a premonition back then of where I would be living today, I probably would have prayed a lot harder to St. Jude, patron of hopeless causes. Our Connecticut cottage is a cross between an English pub, a Vermont barn, and a chicken shed.

Psychometry as a Tool

In my first attempts at giving a psychic reading, I discovered that psychometry acted as a valuable tool. Since psychometry is simply "object reading," the theory is that it is possible to hold someone's personal object, like a ring or watch, and pick up its vibrations. From the vibrations of the object, you may be able to obtain information not otherwise known to you. A single object could literally tell a whole story.

This may sound a bit far-fetched. But keep in mind that Edgar Cayce postulated some thirty years before modern physicists that everything, whether table, tree, flower, bird, or human, has a vibration. From there it is not too difficult to conceive of how a ring someone is wearing could hold recorded life events, as if it were a computer memory.

Ten years ago when John and I were researching *The Ghost of Flight 401*, we used psychometry in an effort to find evidence regarding the crash and the appearances of the dead flight engineer. At the time neither of us was convinced that psychometry could bring results, but on the advice of two Eastern Airlines pilots who were fully developed psychic mediums, we gave it a try. We hired an airboat to take us deep into the swampy Everglades to the site of the crash so that we could collect a number of objects that could be used in a psychometry experiment.

The scene was eerie and depressing. Sprouting out from beneath the muddy water were torn pieces of the wrecked fuselage. Sprinkled everywhere were plastic cups with the airline logo, leather magazine covers, coffee pots, and plastic dishes. From just beneath the water I fished out an empty plastic credit-card holder. John pulled part of an armrest section from a passenger's seat out of the muck. It read: "Push for comfort, music, lights."

We put twelve objects into separate heavy brown envelopes. No one could tell what the contents were. As a control, I put objects that had nothing to do with the crash into three envelopes. Then we delivered the fifteen envelopes to a group of parapsychology students who knew nothing of the contents or our purpose.

The students sat in a circle, each clutching a brown envelope. Their eyes were closed. They looked almost as if they were about to fall asleep. After about ten minutes they began to write down the information they had received. One result was incredible:

An airplane lands in water.

A missing person.

Feel as if I am close to the airport, close to a canal.

I see lights, like those of an airport, then I don't see them anymore.

Feel a pain in the forehead and eyes.

There is a very restless spirit at the crash site and will not rest until his mother knows about spiritual things. She told him but he didn't believe her. Now he does.

I see lights as if I am near an airport, then I don't see them.

I feel a pain in the face, a sick feeling.

Two planes at night, one following another.

Male voice saying my mother told me about this but I didn't believe her. She must stop working so hard and she must stop worrying so much. I have seen the light. . . . Now I believe.

Somebody must tell her.

Please tell her not to cry. I believe.

Equally interesting was the student who got one of the control envelopes. The envelope contained my charm bracelet, which I had since I was seven years old. The following is what the student wrote:

I see a doll

A gold cross

Something significant about September

A pair of slippers

I get something silly like Mickey Mouse

I see a gun but no violence

There's a horse

Right down the line, the psychometry reading was on target. The bracelet held a charm of a little girl holding a doll. There was a charm of a gold cross that I got for my first Holy Communion. There was a September birthstone. Although there was no charm of slippers alone, the bracelet held a tiny charm of Cinderella. There was a charm of Mickey Mouse ears. The most interesting part of the reading was the last two things the student wrote: "I see a gun but no violence," and "there's a horse." My brother had given me a charm of the Lone Ranger, his outstretched hand holding a gun. And of course the Lone Ranger was on his faithful horse, Silver.

The most convincing case for psychometry, however, is

made when you try for yourself and receive accurate information that you had no conscious way of knowing. This happened to me. About a year after that first experiment with the airplane parts, Guy Playfair, a writer and researcher for the British Society of Psychical Research, asked if I would try a psychometry experiment.

Psychometry at Work

Only hours after John and I had arrived in London for the British publisher's promotion of *The Ghost of Flight* 401, Guy Playfair phoned our hotel room. He said that he had just read John's book, learned of my sudden psychic development, and wondered if I would help investigate a dramatic poltergeist case. Poltergeists are reported to be spirits who make noise, throw objects, rap walls, and generally cause havoc.

He asked me to help because he wanted a psychic view from an outsider who had no prior knowledge of the case. And since John and I had been in town only a matter of hours, he thought it would be most unlikely that we would know anything about it. He was right. We knew nothing.

Within an hour of our phone conversation, Playfair arrived at our hotel with a sealed envelope. I sat down in a large Queen Anne chair with the envelope resting on my lap. Then I closed my eyes and began to regulate my breathing pattern as I did in meditation. I continued this rhythmic breathing for ten minutes, all the while trying to imagine myself becoming lighter and lighter and going higher and higher until I felt as if my physical body had begun to blend with the surroundings. When this happened I knew I had reached an altered state of consciousness and that my channel was open to receive psychic information.

Once I was in this state, I silently asked to be provided with answers concerning the contents of the envelope. As always, I reminded myself I would be a channel only for positive purposes. Then I imagined myself bathed in a spiritual white light of protection.

The idea of opening yourself as a channel for only positive energies is Edgar Cayce's bottom line. He tells us that we must live in body and mind so that we may be a channel through which the Creative Forces flow. Cayce believed that if we followed this advice the natural consequences would be psychic manifestations.

After a few moments I began to receive impressions of the contents of the manila envelope. The best way I can describe the impressions is to say that images began to unroll on a movie screen in my mind's eye. Suddenly I saw a street sign, Wood Lane. Next I saw two women, an older one and a younger one. I sensed the name Rose. I got an image of a red brick house with green trim. Then as quickly as the information flowed, it stopped.

I immediately looked toward Playfair for his reaction. He had none. I wasn't sure if his marked lack of expression was due to British reserve or if he was thinking, Take her back to the rubber room and give her her shots. After a few moments of blank staring, he asked if he could use the phone.

Later he confided that he had been so startled at the accuracy of the information that he had to phone the British Society for Psychical Research to make sure that nobody there had tipped me off to the contents of the envelope. The house was on Wood Lane. It was red brick trimmed in green. Two women lived in the house, a mother and daughter. The mother's name was Rose.

The next afternoon in a cold, drizzling rain we visited the house where the poltergeist activity had taken place.

The rooms were in a frightful mess. Radiators were ripped out from the wall. A sofa had turned 360 degrees. All had been photographed by the police. The daughter had been thrown from her bed onto a dresser. There had been constant rumblings through the night. The family understandably moved out. They were never bothered by poltergeist activity again.

Group Psychometry

Now that you are familiar with psychometry, let's try a group experiment. Invite up to a half-dozen people to your home. Ask them to bring a special object of importance, such as a class ring or a favorite watch or necklace. Have the group sit comfortably and begin a fifteen-minute meditation, following Cayce's deep breathing process to clear the mind of all distractions.

After this select two volunteers—one to be a reader and one to be a subject. Ask the subject to pass the token object to the reader. Instruct the reader to hold the object and allow a free flow of impressions to come into his or her mind. Have the reader write down all the impressions he or she receives, regardless of how unrelated they may seem.

Once this is done, have the reader read the notes aloud. Now ask the subject to confirm all those impressions that have any kind of meaning in his or her life. It is important to point out at the start that the reading is not about the object itself but about the total person, because the object carries the overall information of the subject's life, as if it's a microchip.

Now select two more volunteers and repeat the process until everybody has had a chance to be a reader or a reader and subject. After this open the group up for a general discussion on what has taken place. Remember that Cayce firmly believed that group effort was an effective way to reinforce psychic capacity. It would be interesting to note the percentage of correct impressions to confirm the effectiveness of this facet of psychic development.

Remote Viewing

Several days after my psychometry experiment with Guy Playfair, a physicist from the University of London contacted me. He had heard about the experiment with Guy Playfair and wanted to know if I would be willing to participate in a remote viewing experiment.

As mentioned, remote viewing is simply what it says it is—viewing at a distance. While in an altered state of consciousness induced by meditation, you attempt to project your mind to perceive certain far-off events. They could be feet away or thousands of miles away.

A correspondent once asked Cayce how he could project his awareness to a specific locality to observe events there. Cayce replied that time and space are not limited by physical elements on earth. He said that just as the conscious mind can visualize a picture of an incident that has happened in time, so can the spiritual mind project itself and be conscious of events at other locations. He added that these occurrences come as flashes to the conscious mind and that they may gradually be sustained as one develops.

I was looking forward to the remote viewing experiment, mostly to satisfy my growing curiosity of the psychic world. Each time I had success with an experiment, I gained more confidence and quieted the nagging fear that I was just putting one over on myself. Edgar Cayce said that one of the keys to furthering psychic development is believing in our psychic capabilities. Fear, anxiety, and skepticism, he said, blocked the psychic channel. The best way I found to believe in my psychic ability was to test the information that came through for accuracy.

Since remote viewing is not exactly a highly valued skill in the material world, I had to keep reminding myself that it is possible. The idea of time and space is a concept we have constructed with our finite minds—at least that is what modern science is telling us today and Cayce said more than fifty years ago.

My first experiment in remote viewing took place several days after the physicist first phoned. At a specified date and time I was to stop whatever I was doing, sit down, and concentrate on projecting my mind to the location where the physicist was. Without a clue of where he would be or what he would be doing, I was supposed to psychically perceive events taking place.

At the designated time I sat down and cleared my mind of all distractions. With my eyes closed I began to regulate my breathing to achieve an altered state of consciousness. As I continued the breathing I tried to imagine myself as only light without a physical body. After about ten minutes I felt that familiar sensation of lifting above myself and blending with my surroundings. Then I imaged the physicist in my mind's eye and asked my higher self to show me where he was and what he was doing.

On the mental movie screen I saw him sitting in a chair. Although I had never been to his home, I felt he was at home, not at the university, even though it was two o'clock in the afternoon on a weekday. He was wearing a red plaid shirt. Off to his left was a telephone. On his right I saw a desk with something that looked like a paper mobile on it. Above the desk I saw a shelf with lots of books. There was a white car in the driveway. I sensed the presence of a woman in the house.

That evening the physicist phoned. He had been at home. He was not wearing a red plaid shirt, but he was sitting against a red plaid blanket that had been draped over the chair. There was a telephone on his right—not his left. The desk was on his left—not his right. He said that I might have seen a mirror image of the phone and desk.

There was no mobile on his desk. There was however a stack of crumpled papers. He said that from a distance they might resemble a paper mobile. He went on to say that there was no bookshelf above his desk, but there were stacks of books lined along his desk that reached practically to the ceiling. A beige car was in the driveway, not white. The car belonged to a woman friend who had dropped by unexpectedly.

I didn't score 100 percent, but nevertheless I was amazed by the results and by the confirmation that I wasn't just imagining I had psychic ability. The physicist seemed quite pleased with the results. I had scored above 80 percent. Just when I was starting to think how wonderful I was, he said that my high score was not that unusual. Many people who have never before had an experience with the psychic score very high on the remote viewing experiment. I asked why. He thought that we might all have latent ability to perceive events outside our physical bodies.

This is what Cayce said: Our mental and spiritual forces may manifest without a physical body.

The following day I participated in another remote viewing experiment. This time the physicist set up the test with a student. I was given only a photograph, no other information. As with the first experiment, I was instructed to concentrate on projecting my mind to the location of the student. I scored 90 percent. This was enough to tempt me to hang a shingle on my door: Remote Viewer.

A very convincing instance of remote viewing happened to a houseguest of ours, Nima. He was a young Sherpa guide who had preserved our lives during a precarious trek to the base camp of Mount Everest in the Himalayas. Because he was suffering from advanced tuberculosis that could not be cured there, we brought him back to Connecticut where American doctors saved him. The six months that Nima spent with us provided deep insight into Eastern philosophy. When Nima wasn't glued to his new-found friend, the television, he would often show flashes of startling mystical prowess.

One day Nima and I had just returned from shopping. We were unloading the groceries from the car when Nima suddenly paled.

"Mother sick," Nima blurted out. At the same time, he clutched his stomach as if he were struck with a sharp pain.

"What makes you say that?" I asked, thinking that he was just homesick. Nima was very close to his mother. That morning we had gone to five different shoe stores in search of the warmest and best-looking boots for his mother.

"Nima see mother in head," he said, pointing to his forehead. "Mother on floor in bed. Spirit A-Tutu with mother. Nima scared."

My first impulse was to pick up the phone and call Nima's home. But that was impossible. There were no phones near the foot of Mount Everest where Nima's family lived. John and I decided to telegraph the expedition outfitter Nima worked for in Kathmandu. Possibly they could arrange for a runner to get a message to Nima's home. A runner would take a week or two.

One month later, Nima's "remote viewing" incident was confirmed in a letter written by his father. Nima's mother had indeed been seriously ill. Just as Nima said, Spirit A-Tutu, the local shaman, had been summoned to perform an elaborate ritual to exorcise the "evil spirits" from her body, returning her high temperature to normal.

Amazingly, all this took place on the exact day Nima

saw it happen. I asked Nima if he often saw these types of things. He said he always knew when there was a problem and told me that when his close friend was killed on an Everest expedition he saw him lying in an ice crevasse. I often wondered if Nima's ability to see things happen was because he had no telephones or other modern clutter to rely on. If so, maybe that is why psychic phenomenon does not come so readily for Westerners. Everywhere we turn we are overloaded with stimuli bombarding our senses.

Group Experiment: Remote Viewing

Remote viewing consists of the ability to "see" events taking place at another physical location. Let's give it a try. Keep in mind that Cayce said that our conscious mind can project itself at will through our spiritual mind. I know that I always have to keep reminding myself that all this really works. As my uncle Bud says, "There's a fine line between those who are operating with a full deck and those who are collecting bean dip recipes."

Once again, the ideal number of people to invite to your home for this experiment is about half a dozen. When everyone is comfortable, ask for a volunteer to go into another room. If there's time, the volunteer may even get in his or her car and drive to another location. It is of course crucial that nobody in the group knows where the volunteer is going.

Meanwhile, lead the group into a fifteen-minute meditation following Cayce's method of deep breathing to help separate the conscious mind from the unconscious. As your guests meditate, instruct them to keep a mental picture of the volunteer in their minds at all times.

You, as leader, may remind the group that the mental

image of the volunteer is becoming more and more three-dimensional. Now instruct the members of the group to feel as if they are in the same surroundings as the volunteer. They can begin to sense a different room or place, with the colors coming into view, with the shapes and contours of the surroundings appearing in full three-dimensional form. Is it cooler? Is it warmer? Is the volunteer sitting, standing, lying down, or walking? Tell the group members to feel as if they could reach out and touch the volunteer.

After about ten or fifteen minutes of this visualization, ask the group members to remove themselves from the mental image of the volunteer and take a few deep breaths through the nose and exhale slowly through the mouth. Then have them open their eyes and write down the images they received, as ridiculous as they may sound. During an experiment at our house one person wrote down that she saw the volunteer in a zoo, but she knew that the volunteer could not have reached a zoo in only fifteen minutes. Actually the volunteer was in my son's room lying on his bed next to a four-foot stuffed chimpanzee on one side and a stuffed giraffe on the other!

Of course you may improvise this experiment to suit your wishes. It might be interesting to have a friend or spouse who is on a vacation or a business trip try remote viewing. You both should keep track of the exact times and locations of various events so that you can check for accuracy.

If all this sounds too fantastic for serious minds, remember that astronaut Edgar Mitchell conducted a series of planned remote viewing experiments when he was in outer space! Some were successful, and his intense interest in psychic studies continues.

Enter Telepathy

Another aspect of extrasensory perception is telepathy. Telepathy is the ability to communicate directly from one person's mind to another's without using the five senses. This phenomenon is the most frequently experienced form of E.S.P. reported by members of the A.R.E. It is the capacity to send and receive mental pictures, sounds, and words that are at times as reliable as impressions sent through conventional means of communication.

Steps to Telepathy

Edgar Cayce believed that telepathy is a skill that could be developed in a few weeks. His instructions were simple and to the point: Choose a partner with whom you feel comfortable, perhaps a friend or member of your family. It is best if the person you choose is not likely to be near for at least three hours before the experiment. This is to ensure that the information your receive comes from E.S.P. and not from conscious recall of what you have just heard.

After you have chosen a partner, agree on the time of day you will experiment. Cayce suggested that you set aside at least ten minutes at the same time each day. If your schedules do not allow for this, it is okay to vary the time. It is essential, however, that you do the exercise every day for at least twenty consecutive days.

At the agreed-upon time, sit down and clear your mind of all distractions. As mentioned earlier, it is important to get rid of all negative emotions. Fear, worry, anxiety, frustration, hate, and anger will block the psychic channel.

Positive emotions, such as love, on the other hand, will act as a direct conduit to your higher self.

Once in a positive frame of mind, perform the simple head roll exercise. This will help relieve tension and stress that can also block your psychic channel. Then with a straight spine, focus on an affirmation or mantra or both. This will aid in separating you from the physical. At the same time, begin Cayce's method of deep breathing to accelerate an altered state of consciousness. Breathe deeply through the right nostril. Hold the breath for a moment, then exhale through the mouth. Next inhale through the left nostril and exhale through the right nostril, keeping the mouth closed. As you inhale, imagine that you are pulling strength into your body. If you feel the need, you may close the nostril not being used with a finger.

As you continue this breathing pattern, imagine your mind to be a blank screen. Now place your partner on the screen. What is your partner doing? What is she wearing? How does she feel? Is she tired? Is she preoccupied with other thoughts? What are those thoughts? Do you feel as if she is sending you a specific message? Why don't you try sending her a message? Imagine your message leaving your physical body and traveling through space and time to your friend. A rough comparison might be made to the way a radio signal can be bounced off cloud layers to send or receive messages at great distance. But the psychic requires no electronic boosters. It operates in the spiritual sphere beyond the laws of physics.

As your mental screen begins to show images, jot them down. At first you may think that everything you're writing is just your imagination. This is why it is important to keep doing this exercise each day for several weeks. After a week or so you'll be able to distinguish between a legitimate E.S.P. experience and your imagination.

Beyond the Conscious Mind

I don't blame you if you're thinking, big deal, why bother with all of this? The experiments are not an end, but a beginning. They are tools to help reveal our true nature. These tests demonstrate that if we are able to perceive information outside our conscious selves, then we are capable of achieving more.

Cayce said that there is no limit. We have access to virtually all knowledge once we learn how to tap into the greater unconscious. These experiments are simply instruments to help us alter our view of reality, making vast new opportunities available to us.

Living only in our conscious self is akin to living in a closet at Versailles. But by stepping out into its spacious galleries we can explore the richness of all the rooms. Why then do so many of us remain in the closet? Cayce felt it is because we are hemmed in by old belief patterns concerning who we are and what we are capable of achieving. We are products of reflected appraisal. Before a child gets out of elementary school his future is often labeled. I know mine was.

I remember Sister Mary Agnes wrote in my eighth-grade autograph book that when I grew up I'd have a dozen kids and they would all be Hoola Hoop champions. It was her way of saying that was the best I could hope for. Fortunately, through the exploration of my higher self, the curse of the little old lady who lived in the shoe never materialized. I was able to expand my horizon by dipping into the Cosmic Pool that is available to all who choose it.

Setting a Goal

Before we move on it is important to review the aim of our psychic development. Our ultimate goal should be the growth of our spiritual selves. Our will is a reflection of our desires and should be directed for the most creative and unselfish of purposes. Edgar Cayce always contacted the Universal Source; therefore his psychic power was always used constructively. His will, heart, and mind were set on an idealistic goal.

What about your goal? Do you have one? Is it clear or vague in your mind? Can you express it to a friend or even to yourself? Cayce believed that goals were an important motivating force to give direction to our lives. Is your goal worthwhile? Emerson said: "Be careful of what you want, for you will get it." If you have your goal, then Cayce said that you should start from where you are. You must not indulge in vague wishful thinking. Now is the time to begin.

One creative exercise to help convert your goal from abstract to concrete is to write it down. As you do so, write more from intuition than from reason because your intuition springs from the conscious and unconscious levels and is less inhibited. Put down as many details as possible. When you have finished, read over what you have written. As you read, picture yourself as having already accomplished what you want. Once you have this visualization clearly in mind, take the first step. Cayce said: "Forget the past. Forget, forgive and begin where you are" (3674–1).

Acting on Cayce's advice, we'll take our next step forward to explore in depth the mystery of the unconscious mind and its inner connection with both the cosmos and untold minds on the astral plane.

CHANNELING

Beyond This Life

One of the most baffling events of psychic development is called channeling. This happens with the conscious mind of a psychic suspended, and words and information are received that seem to be those of an entity no longer living.

The psychic then becomes a channel, a conduit, an instrument like a radio, not speaking for the self but for a discarnate entity, often with verifiable details that identify the entity clearly as one who is no longer living but still a distinct personality aware of what is going on in both the material and spiritual worlds.

How can this possibly happen? If channeling is real, the only answer is that we don't die after physical death, but live on in an astral state. Many people feel that channeling is distinct evidence of an astral body or soul that lives on.

Life Is Continuous

Edgar Cayce revealed that there is no such thing as death. It is only a transition into the spiritual plane, which in turn is the true reality. Life is continuous. We simply move through another door in a smooth transition.

Many of us have trouble conceiving of this. I know that I used to have great trouble picturing a formless state with no physical body to support a brain and mind. Every time I used to try to imagine myself dead, I pictured myself as the ghost Marion in the television show "Topper."

Cayce told us that we could exist in the "superconsciousness" and retain full self-awareness. The material plane is merely a shadow of the spiritual plane. Just as we are born into the material world, we are born into the spiritual. While we are being born, we have no consciousness of the process. This emerges slowly as we learn and experience. So it is with death. We begin with a new learning experience as we progress in the spiritual realm. "A death in the flesh," said Cayce, "is a birth into the realm of another experience" (989–2).

Our physical body has simply become a discarded shell. An astral body takes its place. Death is birth. "The passing in, the passing out, is as but the summer, the fall, the spring," Cayce told us (281–16). Once we have made the transition into the astral world, our astral body seeks to become at one with its source.

At the same time, the astral body (or soul) can communicate with like minds, either living or dead, just as Cayce did on earth. Cayce visualized that the soul body is made up of "thought atoms" and that the communication coming through a psychic channel is done on a thought-to-thought basis.

Psychic Communication

Cayce pointed out that the physical plane is simply one level of consciousness, a part of the whole, like a room in a house. But psychic communication can override the gap if there is a desire and if there is attunement on both planes.

With this type of communication in mind, I thought back fifteen years to a visit I once had with my grandmother. We had been sitting at her kitchen table nibbling on a chocolate cake. Suddenly my grandmother got up and led me into her bedroom.

She pointed to a photo of my grandfather, who had died several years earlier, and dropped her voice to a whisper usually reserved for gossip. She said that she was about to tell me something she had never told anyone. Sometimes when she was sound asleep she was awakened by my grandfather calling to her. She even imitated the way he would call. I could have done without the eerie sound effects. As it was, I got the chills just hearing her say things like that.

I listened as she told me that my discarnate grandfather would ask about his family. He was concerned that we were all okay. After a polite length of time, I changed the subject. It really hurt to hear my grandmother sound as if she were from La-La Land.

That was fifteen years ago. Today, however, I am able to conceive of life after death. I recently came across an interesting concept of how we might exist after death. The late H. H. Price, professor of logic at Oxford, draws a comparison between life after death and our dreams. Here is a place outside of physical space where you have buildings, fields, mountains, cities, clothing, feelings, sight, and other people you could communicate with. In a vivid dream these are just as real as when you are awake. You can see clearly without the use of your retina. You can hear without the use of your ears. You can experience very real emotions.

Removing the Mystery

To me Professor Price's dream concept made it possible to visualize Edgar Cayce's theory of a life after death and helped make it comprehensible in a literal way.

The Edgar Cayce Foundation and the A.R.E. affiliate constantly receive letters from people who experience spontaneous signs of channeling. Such experiences for those who have little knowledge of parapsychology can be very disturbing. They feel lost, confused, lonely, and set apart from their friends and families. Not many realize that the psychic is an integral part of our everyday lives.

Cayce emphasized that the experiences are not as mystical and occult as they seem. We are all, living and deceased, bathed in the same Universe. Our job is to harmonize with it and understand it. Channeling is striking evidence of this; human minds, living and dead, transcend their infinite bonds and reach out to one another in selective contact. Whatever information comes through in spontaneous or directed efforts can be of great value in our personal lives if we keep always to the desire for the highest and best to come through. There are lower and undeveloped entities that can come through, and they are to be evaluated as such and discarded through the continued reaching for the highest Spiritual Sources.

One inquirer asked Cayce if it was possible for the body of Edgar Cayce to communicate with anyone who has passed into the spirit world. His reply was: "The spirit of all that have passed from the physical plane remain about this plane until their development carries them onward or are returned for their development here; when they are in the plane of communication or remain within this sphere, any may be communicated with'' (3744–2).

Of course, in order to understand the phenomenon of channeling, you have to get yourself to the point where you can believe it. It wasn't until my own experience that I found channeling credible at all. I received messages purporting to come from Benjamin Franklin.

The first time the apparent personality of Franklin came through was quite spontaneous. I was helping my husband do some research on Arthur Conan Doyle at the University of London library. I was tired and had difficulty staying awake. It was hot and stuffy inside despite a drizzling rain and chilly temperatures outside. While I was making notes, my mind wandered. Suddenly my hand began to pick up speed. I was still looking at a Doyle letter, but the words my hand scribbled in my notebook had nothing to do with Doyle.

It happened so quickly I didn't have time to question what was going on. It felt as if someone had his hand over mine and was guiding the pen. But no one was around. This strange writing probably took several minutes, although time seemed to have been suspended. John, who had been away in another part of the library stacks, came back just as my hand came to rest. I deciphered the scrawl. The most interesting part referred to the subject of life after death, which was the subject of Doyle's letter. The scrawl that my hand had written read: "To lack faith is to lack life."

What was confusing was that I had received a strong and indelible impression that the person directing my hand was named Franklin. I didn't know anyone named Franklin.

To confirm the validity of the material I began to speak the messages into a tape recorder. Whenever I tried an altered state, someone who called himself Franklin was mentally making himself known. I tried to ignore it. I was convinced that my imagination was conjuring up that name.

On one quiet December evening we got out our tape deck to see what might come through in the way of general advice concerning a new book John was working on. Nothing so mundane came through. I got that overwhelming "Franklin feeling" again.

I began to speak words entirely out of my cadence. I asked myself: Am I going out of my mind? Is there really someone named Franklin trying to speak through me? John's new book involved the psychic, and I knew he was hoping to get some cosmic guidance if anything was available. My voice on the tape surprised me as much as it surprised John.

"Stage One," my voice spoke on the tape. "Purely on the physical plane. It encompasses the realities as we see them and can be related to others on the physical plane through books, lectures, demonstrations, and readings."

My voice on the tape went on. "Stage Two, or psychic scientific development. This includes the psi factors which are all enveloping. They are part of the holistic approach. They are fundamentally understood when one is in the higher realm of reality."

John asked who was speaking through me. I told him again that it was someone who called himself Franklin. Then the words purporting to come from this entity pronounced: "There is a gaseous cloud all around the Universe and this is preventing communication. Only at times are we able to enter into this cloud formed by energies released from other galaxies. Only when powerful rays are shot through the atmosphere are you able to see on a physical level other levels of reality such as psychic phenomenon and extra-terrestrials. Preparation is being made from other realities to enter a unified dimension and learn other techniques, other realms of importance."

All I knew was that none of this was from my conscious mind or my memory. I broke in on the tape and said to John, "This is really weird stuff. I think this is just my unconscious mind rattling this stuff off. I think I'm just playing little games and I can't function like that."

The tape ended here. What bothered me most about all of this was that people who "hear voices" are the same people who get regular shock treatment. John is not a scientist, but he is scientifically informed as a journalist. In the past ten years he has written three science books and several major articles in science magazines. He couldn't detect anything that was scientifically valid on the tape. My own scientific interest ended when television's "Mr. Wizard" went off the air in the late 1950s.

But just a few days after this incident John ran across a very interesting scientific paper that brought us up sharply. It confirmed almost exactly what the voice of this mysterious character Franklin had scooped out of my unconscious.

A lecturer in mathematics at the University of London wrote: "There is a real paradox associated with rich clusters of galaxies. They do not seem to be gravitationally bound by the matter we see in them. The velocities of the galaxies ought to be fast enough for them to escape from the cluster causing matter, dwarf galaxies, etc., to bind the cluster. The most popular candidate is residual intergalactic gas. There is evidence for such gas, both from its X-ray emission and from its effect on radio sources. This leads naturally to the question of general intercluster gas."

What was puzzling to me was that this confirmed some of the cryptic message that had come through me in the words of Franklin. I wish I had known more about Edgar Cayce at the time because I would have at least been prepared for what was to happen and for better understanding what these strange spontaneous experiences were all about.

Cayce's premise is firm. He said the soul of the individual lives on with full consciousness of existence. This concept may be hard to accept, perhaps because the phenomenon is so overpowering as to be beyond words. But he strongly pointed out in many of his readings that we all have the potential to communicate with other realities and can use it for the benefit of ourselves and others.

Cayce made contact with other realities by releasing his mind from the physical body. In doing so he moved into different levels of consciousness where the highest Spiritual Sources put him in contact with other entities, living or dead, who wanted to communicate.

We All Have the Potential

Cayce said that in our psychic development we should reach for this goal: to become a direct channel for the highest Spiritual Source. Of course when anyone reports a purported psychic contact with a famous personality like Franklin, he or she is likely to be nominated for the Hall of Zanies. Nevertheless I still claim my sanity. Whenever doubts creep in, I remind myself of that national survey on paranormal experiences that was recently conducted by Father Andrew Greeley. You may recall that the survey showed that nearly half of all American adults believe that they have been in contact with someone who has died.

"Such paranormal experiences are generally viewed as hallucinations or symptoms of mental disorder," writes Father Greeley. "But if these experiences were signs of mental illness, our numbers would show the country is going nuts. What was paranormal is now normal. It's even happening to elite scientists and physicians who insist such things cannot possibly happen."

He goes on to say that the survey also revealed that the people who have had these experiences were anything but "religious nuts" or "psychiatric cases." Most, he says, are ordinary Americans who are somewhat above the norm in intelligence and education and somewhat less than average in religious involvement.

"We tested people," Father Greeley says, "who'd had some of the deeper mystical experiences. They were high on the scale of psychological well-being with healthy personalities. The mystics scored at the top."

What does all this add up to? According to Father Greeley, many of these people experiencing some facet of the paranormal have become profoundly trusting, convinced that something good rules in the world. And that, he feels, can have a lasting effect on the world.

And what does this have to do with channeling? I have come to believe through my own experiences and those of others that if we are properly guided along a constructive path to our higher consciousness, we may find evidence of a control coming through as a channel. If you do, you may benefit by learning how that sort of event was handled by a famous psychic such as Jane Roberts. Like Edgar Cayce, she was genuinely puzzled.

Enter Seth

Ten years ago when John and I were preparing for our trip to the Himalayas, we began reading the Seth material that had been channeled through the medium Jane Roberts. Seth used Jane Roberts's voice as a conduit to express wisdom, intelligence, and insight from other realms of existence.

In an effort to learn more about this phenomenon, John wrote to Jane Roberts explaining my sudden psychic development while researching *The Ghost of Flight 401* and how puzzling it was as it continued to escalate. He hoped that she could shed some light on all of this and asked if we could meet at a time convenient for her.

I thought it was a bit presumptuous to assume Jane Roberts would have the inclination or the time to explain psychic phenomenon for two strangers. But one week later she phoned and invited us to come to her home. She said that she had read *The Ghost of Flight 401* and that it would be fascinating to share experiences.

The anticipation of unearthing clues as to why I suddenly developed psychic ability was heightened by the fact that I was actually going to meet the woman who channeled the brilliance of Seth.

It was late August 1978 when we arrived at Jane Roberts's home. Jane and her husband, Robert, lived in a modest attractive Victorian, reminiscent of the turn-of-the-century homes that line many main streets in small American towns. Robert greeted us at the door. He was quietly cordial and pleasant looking.

Jane was sitting in a rocking chair reading a book when we came into the living room. The moment she saw us she dropped her book to the coffee table, leaned forward, and gave us a weak handshake but a hearty welcome. She was much more friendly than I had expected. That was another thing. I always expected psychics to be very standoffish—as if the only people they really cared about were those who have been planted under granite.

"You look just like the photos on the back of your book jackets," Jane said to John.

"Yeah, as if he's going into the jungle to meet Dr. Livingston," I added.

Jane and her husband were quick to laugh, a fact that made them more believable. There was no small talk. Somehow that didn't seem to be necessary. As Jane began asking questions about our research on flight 401, I studied her face. Although she would not stand out in a crowd, her eyes were wide and expressive with an added spirited quality.

We must have talked about our research for close to an hour when Jane said, "Liz, you must have been quite surprised to find yourself suddenly psychic."

I told Jane that was putting it mildly. When I first began to receive messages apparently from the dead flight 401 engineer, I was convinced that either I was making the whole thing up unconsciously or it was time for the men in the white ice cream suits to haul me off. But later when the messages were confirmed by the pilot's widow, I had no choice but to accept that something was going on that I couldn't explain. This left me both intrigued and scared. I didn't understand. Why me? Why now? And what was I supposed to do with this new-found ability? Then I started receiving the automatic handwriting and direct voice channeling from someone called Franklin. It all seemed so preposterous. How could any rational person actually believe in life after death?

I went on to tell Jane and Robert that even as a kid I had difficulty with the concepts of heaven, hell, purgatory, and limbo taught in my Catholic school.

Jane said, "Liz, I think we have something in common."

"You mean you were raised as a Catholic, too?" I asked.

"I was," Jane said. "But by the time I went to college I left heaven, hell, devils, and angels behind. I just couldn't conceive of an all-loving God who could tolerate a devil torturing some unlucky chap in hell. But I didn't spend a lot of time dwelling on the inequity of it all. I had other interests to occupy my mind."

"Jane was a poet. And I'm an artist," Robert said. He was just coming back into the living room carrying a tray of iced tea. "Although we weren't conventionally religious, we did have a relationship with nature."

"Rob and I only went to church for weddings and funerals," Jane added lightly as she cleared the coffee table.

"Suddenly we had to face the possibility of other realities," Jane said. "Before Seth, I had prided myself on the fact that I was an intelligent, open-minded freethinker who didn't allow for such absurdities. Now I look back and realize that this 'open attitude' only extended as far as my fixed notion of what I believed was possible. My thinking was really quite confined. When Seth first made contact I was certain that Seth was something I had cooked up in my subconscious. But there comes a point when you have to look at the facts. And the facts were that an entity called Seth was supplying Rob and me with voluminous knowledge that went far beyond our conscious knowledge. Seth's concepts, cadence, and character are entirely different from mine."

Jane spoke of Seth as if he were an old friend who lived down the road. Had I not experienced a similar type of contact with the dead flight engineer, I probably would have left. But my contact with the engineer over the twelve months of research had become so real that I often found myself speaking about him in the present tense.

What interested me most was that Seth had initially made contact with Jane through the old-fashioned Ouija board. This is the same way John and I had contacted the flight engineer. The Ouija board is a well-known device about the size of a desk blotter. It has the alphabet and numbers from one to ten on it. Separate from the board is a small plastic indicator on three legs with a window in the center. The theory behind the Ouija board is that when two people place their fingers lightly on the indicator, a Spiritual Force causes the indicator to move without conscious volition of the operators, gliding to letters that can spell out words and even sentences.

John was turned off about the idea of experimenting with a Ouija board. He argued that he wanted to keep the book on an "investigative-journalistic level." However, I was able to convince him that we should give it a try.

The week we went to buy the board, John's latest book on nuclear power had just come out. Because of this, John stood at the opposite end of the store as I paid for the Ouija board. He was paranoid that someone would see him with it and think that he did all of his research on a Ouija board.

When we got home and tried it, John accused me of moving the indicator. I accused him of the same thing. It is a strange sensation to have your fingers resting on an inanimate object that suddenly begins to glide from one letter to another. Often the indicator moved so swiftly we barely had time to call off the letters into a tape recorder.

Out of this experiment came a sense of truth, a sense of validity that we couldn't deny. The dead flight engineer began to emerge as real. I couldn't explain it. John couldn't explain it. But somehow a personality was sending us clear messages that were later fully confirmed.

I was deep in thoughts of how Seth too had first emerged over the Ouija board when suddenly I was jolted back to the present. Without warning, soft-spoken and mild-mannered Jane Roberts bellowed: "Good afternoon!" It was unmistakably the voice of Seth.

Seth Speaks Out

"You question your psychic nature, my friend?" Seth asked through Jane. Her voice was so loud and forceful that I could hardly believe it came from such a petite woman. Her features had suddenly lost their softness, taking on an almost masculine appearance.

Jane's eyes were locked on mine as she waited for my response. I merely nodded. Then I looked toward Jane's husband for his reaction. He took a sip of iced tea as if nothing were out of the ordinary. John was not as casual. He grabbed a pen and notepad from his pocket and began taking notes. I tried to be equally cool, but my heart was doing 180.

"My friend," Seth went on loudly, "it appears you are attempting to perceive the nature of reality without altering your concepts of what reality is. You will only begin to have a depth of true understanding when you comprehend that there are many layers to the individual consciousness. Life is not contingent on a physical form. Our physical beings are the materialization of what we believe we are. If you believe that you are capable of operating in other realms, then you will. If you do not believe in this potential, then you will remain as a three-dimensional being. You project what you are. Those who have moved on from the earth plane project what they are. Although a different form from yours, it is the same. Do you understand?"

"Yes," I said so softly that Seth boomed, "Do you understand?"

"I think so!" I shouted. I hoped that I didn't sound pugnacious.

Seth continued to speak through Jane. "At present it appears that you are creating your own confusion by projecting confusion. You must liberate yourself from what you have been taught reality is. In many respects you are locked in a prison that you have constructed around yourself. But the truth is: You are malleable. You can mold yourself and your surroundings to what you desire. If you desire communication with other realities, then communicate," Seth again boomed, hitting about a nine on the Richter scale.

I glanced at John for his reaction to all of this. He shrugged his shoulders and then went back to taking copious notes.

"Space and time have little to do with reality," Seth continued. "You are not at the mercy of your physical construct, unless of course you desire to be. Do you understand?" Seth asked. Jane's eyes had lost their twinkle. They also seemed to have lost all contact with earth.

"Yes!" I answered loudly and promptly. Then I quickly said, "May I ask a question?"

"You may," Seth said curtly. Jane leaned back in her chair for the first time since Seth had come through. But she still appeared forceful despite her frail frame.

"Actually it's a two-part question," I said apologetically. "One: Was I really in touch with the dead flight 401 engineer? And two: Is Franklin a real entity or is he something I concocted in my imagination?"

Jane lunged forward in her chair. "In the beginning Rupert questioned the validity of what he was receiving, too," Seth began. (Rupert is Seth's name for Jane and Seth always refers to Rupert as *he*.) "It is essential for your own psychic development that you do not ask questions concerning other layers of realities with a single-layer understanding of what reality is. When you are in a mode of communication with other realities, then it is the appropriate time to ask your departed friends if the communication is authentic.

"Let me draw an analogy," Seth continued. "In your physical realm the telephone rings, you pick it up, you share information, then you hang up. Afterwards do you question if the phone really rang? Was the information you heard accurate? Did the person really call or did you just imagine that he did? Of course you wouldn't question the authenticity of what you experienced in the physical realm. Then why do you question your communication with other levels of reality? They are as real as the physical."

"Oh," I said, as if a two-hundred-watt light bulb had suddenly gone on inside my head. Then I got up the nerve to ask one more question. "John and I are preparing for a trip to the Himalayas. Do you think it will be successful?"

"Do you want it to be a success?" Seth asked.

"Yes, very much," I said.

"Then project confidence," Seth said in a thunderous tone that made me flinch. "Keep your channels open. And recognize your unique multidimensional level."

With that, the unseen presence of Seth left. Jane relaxed in her chair, her features once again soft, her manner delicate, her voice affable. Perhaps it was my imagination. But I don't think so. John also claimed he could actually see an abrupt personality shift from Seth back to Jane.

When I returned to Connecticut with John's complete transcript of our meeting with Seth, I received mixed reviews. A few of my more open-minded friends were interested. Most of them, however, read the first line of Seth's communication, groaned, and said something to the effect of: "If they're out there, you'll find them." My Irish-Italian family was about as open to psychic channeling as they were to health food. They didn't buy seven-grain bread, tofu, herbal pasta, or voices from the "other side." In fact, I used to feel the exact same way.

One incident that stands out in my mind as a distinct reminder of how impossible I used to find it to accept all of this happened twenty-five years earlier in an eighth-grade religion class: Sister Mary Agnes turned to Cherry Preuss, who sat two seats in front of me.

"Cherry," the sister said, "how many angels are there?"

"I think there are 679, Sister," Cherry answered, "not counting the archangels, guardian angels, and unfaithful angels."

"That's a very good rough estimate, Cherry," Sister Mary Agnes said. "But the exact number is not known."

"Elizabeth," Sister Mary Agnes said, "do all of our temptations to sin come from unfaithful angels?"

"Yes, Sister," I said as I shoved the movie magazine I had been reading into my desk.

She was quick to respond. "*Wrong*, Elizabeth. All of our temptations to sin do *not* come from the unfaithful angels. Only some of them do," Sister Mary Agnes said. Then she slid some stray strands of gray fuzzy hair into the hood of her habit and asked, "Elizabeth, what does God do to thirteen-year-old girls who idolize movie stars instead of angels?"

I thought a moment then said, "You eventually get run over by one of their Cadillacs?"

"*Exactly,*" she said as she grabbed the movie magazine from inside my desk.

Five minutes later, I was sitting in the rectory, sandwiched between Sister Mary Agnes and Father O'Malley. The movie magazine was on one side of his desk. On the other side was a miniature nativity scene that you shake and it fills with snow.

"Elizabeth," Father O'Malley said as he held up the movie magazine, "why are you attracted to this smut, and not to our beloved angels and saints?"

My first mistake of the day had been to bring the fan magazine to school. My second mistake was to level with Father O'Malley. I told him that I found it hard to imagine saints and angels in heaven on fluffy clouds. When I noticed his face become a wrinkled dumpling, I softened. I said that I really loved all the angels and saints, and I was positive that they were really up there, but I just found it sometimes difficult to devote all my time to praying and adoring them.

"So instead you'd rather adore Frankie Avalon?" he asked. He leafed through the magazine that featured Frankie Avalon and Annette Funicello in bathing suits on the set of their new beach movie.

Before I had a chance to answer, he walked over to his file cabinet and pulled out a wad of holy cards. He began to shuffle through the deck as if he were getting ready to play poker. Finally he dealt me a handful of cards. The laminated plastic depicted everyone from St. Edith, patron of poverty, to St. Jerome, patron of pure thoughts. Each day I was supposed to pray to the saints to take away my earthly desires.

Now almost three decades later, my belief system is more receptive to the supernatural than ever before. This is not to say that I believe in angels bouncing on fluffy clouds somewhere well above thirty-five thousand feet. I believe in the life after death that Cayce spoke of: "Death—as commonly spoken of—is only passing through God's other door. That there is continued consciousness is evidenced, ever, by . . . the abilities of entities to project or to make those impressions upon the consciousness of sensitives." (1472–2).

Had I not had that direct communication with the dead flight engineer, I'm not sure I would be able to accept Cayce's statement without a bit of doubt. But my experience literally lifted a veil from my eyes, revealing a timeless, spaceless world.

There were moments, however, when I wished to go back to my old self—as Seth called it, my "three-dimensional physical reality." In many ways it was more convenient. I wasn't constantly defending my sanity. But all those feelings vanished each time I meditated. Meditation brought a peace and serenity that I had never known before. While in that meditative state I felt as if all problems could be solved, all answers could be found. For the first time in my life I felt as if I was in control. There was some sort of cosmic knowing that I had a power within to achieve virtually whatever I wanted.

The Next Psychic Encounter

In spite of the doubts that would sometimes creep into my thoughts, my psychic development continued literally upward and onward. The next psychic communication happened at eleven thousand feet in the Himalayas. Steven Spielberg could not have dreamed up a better stage set for Franklin to make himself known once again.

Earlier in the day John and I had wheezed up a precarious frozen trail to the Lamjura Pass, choked in fresh snow and thin oxygen. At regular intervals throughout our forty-day trek I reminded myself of Seth's message: "Project confidence. Keep your channels open. Recognize your unique multidimensional level."

I tried to follow this other-worldly advice, but by the third week it wasn't easy. I had blisters the size of balloons on each toe. My left knee felt as if it were a giant Slinky. I lost all confidence and sense of adventure the first time I had to cross a flimsy bamboo bridge decorated with prayer flags to commemorate all those who had lost their lives crossing the bridge.

At sundown we climbed into our six-by-eight geodesic tent. It was pitch dark inside. I lighted a wavering candle and stuck it in an old bottle. I propped myself against a duffel bag, took out my notebook, and began to doodle. My mind filled with the endless bamboo bridges we were constantly forced to cross. There was the distant scream of Himalayan jackals in the distance. The wind was slapping against the sides of the tent. Then my hand began to write without any conscious effort on my part. Again it felt as if another hand were guiding it. Beside me in his sleeping bag, John asked what in the world was I up to. My hand was writing one proverb after another.

Within an hour there were over seventy of them. My hand signed the name "Franklin." To put it mildly, I was perplexed. I had never written a proverb before nor have I since. Here are some of them:

Men of few words, should be.

If you heard it through the grapevine the wine is probably sour.

There are only two types of people who should ponder the past—historians and bores.

The theory of evolution is only partially evolved.

It is the fortunate man who never discusses his misfortunes.

The best neighbors are usually somebody else's.

Whoever said charity begins at home was not an orphan.

Hang on to yesterday, and tomorrow will be duller than today.

He who lives in a world of dreams may be inviting nightmares.

Some of the proverbs reflected the thoughts of Edgar Cayce even though I knew nothing of his vast works at that time:

God has been cast in so many religions, it's amazing He always shows up knowing His lines.

No one religion has a corner on God; He owns the whole block.

In each person is a nugget of God waiting to be mined.

If scientists put physics to music they might strike a new chord.

The rhythm of life is in tune with death, and both are in perfect harmony.

My belief that these proverbs came from Franklin is strengthened by his own epitaph, which also blends with Edgar Cayce's outlook:

When I see nothing annihilated (in the works of God) and not a drop of water wasted, I cannot expect the annihilation of souls, or believe that He will suffer the daily waste of millions of minds ready made that now exist, and put Himself to the continual trouble of making new ones. Thus, finding myself to exist in the world, I believe I shall, in some shape or other, always exist; and, with all the inconveniences human life is liable to, I shall not object to a new edition of mine, hoping, however, that the errata of the last may be corrected. The body of Benjamin Franklin, Printer (like the cover of an old book, its contents torn and stripped of its lettering and gilding), lies here, food for worms; but the work shall not be lost, for it will (as he believed) appear once more in a new and more elegant edition, revised and corrected by the Author.

Benjamin Franklin's
epitaph for himself,
composed in 1728

In an effort to make sure I wasn't deluding myself, I took these proverbs to Dr. Whitfield Bell, the foremost authority on Benjamin Franklin, for his scrutiny. His opinion was that though they had never appeared in Franklin's writings, the style and wit were most definitely in character with his writings. In addition, the *Reader's Digest* research department reported that none of these proverbs had ever been in print, thus eliminating the chance that these had been the result of my unconscious recall.

All this simply convinces me that I have reached beyond my five senses, and you can too. Cayce told us that the individual who gives himself as a channel for a benevolent discarnate entity and for the good of others may indeed be guided or shown the way. He did, however, make a distinction between automatic and inspirational writing, preferring the latter, which springs from the inner self rather than an outer entity. He told us: "The inspirational writing may develop the soul of the individual, while the automatic may rarely reach beyond the force that is guiding or directing" (5752–4).

Simply, Cayce was warning us that we must be careful of whom we contact in automatic writing because the results are only as helpful as the entity guiding us. This is why it is important to preface all such experiments with meditation and prayer, asking to contact only the highest and most constructive sources.

Channeling Experiments to Try

Perhaps you would like to experiment with inspirational writing or automatic writing or direct voice communication. Automatic writing may be difficult in the beginning. Your first step is to clear your mind of all the day's distractions.

Replace all negative thoughts with love, keeping in mind that Cayce said love is the only force that will open psychic channels for constructive purposes.

To help separate yourself from the stresses of the physical world and enter into the spiritual realm, let's review Cayce's head roll exercise: Sit erect with your spine straight. Drop your head forward until your chin rests on your chest. Next bring your head upright to its natural position. Repeat this slowly three times.

Now drop your head back and lift it three times. Tilt your head to the left, bringing your ear close to your shoulder, then bring your head upright; repeat this three times. After you repeat this to the right three times, begin a slow head roll counterclockwise by dropping your chin to your chest and rolling your head completely around until your chin reaches the same position again. Do the head roll clockwise to the right in the same way.

To further release tension, let's try another exercise recommended by Cayce: Tighten the muscles of your toes, feet, and ankles as hard as you can and then suddenly release them. Do the same with your calves. Move up to the knees, thighs, and buttocks. Do the same with your stomach, shoulders, and upper arms. Tighten your neck, jaw, and other facial muscles. Always relax suddenly, like a spring. Now tighten all of your muscles, hold for a moment, and suddenly let go.

At this point it would be a good idea to prepare a pad and pencil and tape recorder so you won't have to break your concentration after our next step, Edgar Cayce's deep meditation, which will enable you to make contact with higher energy forces. As you inhale, picture that you are pulling strength into your body. With each breath imagine yourself lifting above your physical body. Continue this breathing exercise as long as you feel the process is helping you lose your self-awareness. I usually meditate in this way for a minimum of fifteen minutes, but the length of time will vary with the individual.

Envision yourself bathed in a protective spiritual white light. Now ask your higher self that you be used as a channel for *only* positive, creative, and constructive forces. As you do so it is critical that you suspend your conscious mind, relieve yourself of that burden. Soft music in the background might help to relax you, but it isn't necessary. Now hold your pen or pencil lightly over your notepad. Do not consciously move your hand. And don't be anxious for the experience. Anxiety will block your psychic channel.

If your hand begins to write, the result may at first look like scribbling. Go with the flow. It is important not to analyze, judge, or interrupt what your hand is writing until the session is over. Allow yourself a full twenty minutes for the process. If nothing happens during that time, don't feel as if you have wasted your time. You haven't. You have prepared the way for psychic channeling in the future.*

Testing the Spirits

Cayce advised us to "test the spirits" to make sure we are in contact with the most constructive entities, rather than those entities that are unfruitful and unworthy. Cayce felt that much of the testimony of channeling, his own and others', suggests a closeness and communion between benign entities on both planes.

One of Edgar Cayce's readings reveals his thoughts of a dream he had concerning his own death. He related that in

---

*The Edgar Cayce readings suggest caution in exploring this area. I, however, have found this technique helpful.

his dream he found many conditions that, to the material mind, were hard to understand. Within the dream he saw the reflection of the Oneness of the Universal Forces that was manifested through psychic force. The dream revealed to him the realm of the spiritual world, where there was peace and communion of loved ones between the earth's plane and the spiritual world. In his dream, chaos did not rule, but rather the Oneness of purpose and truth did. And when psychic communication, such as channeling, takes place, discarnate entities came to assist in the material plane when allowed to. These Cayce believed were the entities that would enrich our lives in harmony with the creative purposes of the Universe.

Death, however, does not bring immediate spiritual enlightenment. Cayce added that a lot depends on the ability of the discarnate entity to draw on the One Spiritual Force to pass along articulate information from the Cosmic Consciousness. Thoughts can become barriers or steppingstones according to the ability of the medium or the entity to harmonize their vibrations, first in tune with the Cosmic Forces, and then with each other.

Spirit Guides

Cayce indicated the possibility of the psychic encountering of a spiritual guide in the process of channeling. "There are ever, for every soul, those that may be termed the guides or guardian angels" (405–1). He described these guides as protective souls, not celestial beings. There are often reports of such encounters in psychic development. Cayce said there is true guidance available from such entities if we remove the barriers formed by our attachment to the physical plane.

In regard to automatic writing, again Cayce felt that the

results must be tested. This is one reason I extensively researched the Franklin material.

We've noted in this chapter that Cayce assured us there is no such thing as death. In doing so he went beyond the conventional Biblical point of view, and offered an explanation of how and why life after death may be possible.

All this is important to have in mind when and if we encounter channeling. It may come either spontaneously with ourselves, or we may observe such a happening in others. It is of considerable comfort to realize that life after life is possible. This in turn adds meaning to our lives here in the physical world. We've also seen how some personal channeling brings the realization that loved ones who have gone before us are still conscious, living individualities in the spiritual realm and that all of us will also maintain full self-awareness.

Cayce's view that we continue to develop ourselves after leaving the physical body is encouraging. His concept that death is really the same as birth, only in another plane, is also comforting because we have already experienced birth on this plane and have found it to be merely the beginning of life, not the end.

In attempting to develop our own psychic abilities we have learned that we can confirm much of his hopeful and helpful state of affairs and thus enrich our current lives.

Be Still

Cayce's most helpful advice is simple: Be still! This is so easy that it seems ridiculous that we have to remind ourselves to follow the instruction when we start meditation. I remember the old cartoons where a character is rushing toward the edge of a cliff and suddenly stiffens its limbs as it slides to a screeching stop just in time. The pace of modern living requires us to come to that screeching stop to get rid of all the distractions of the day. Only after we force ourselves to come to an abrupt stop can we even begin to release our latent psychic abilities.

Cayce never had a "control" as a middleman for his readings; he went directly to what he called the Universal Superconsciousness, thus taking an express highway to the highest Spiritual Sources. But we have learned that there is always a possibility of a control such as Jane Roberts's Seth coming to speak through the psychic with words of wisdom and insight. The better controls seem to be advanced souls on the spiritual plane that want to guide and help where possible on the physical plane.

Often these controls will reveal the existence of reincarnation and how the past lives of the individual echo in the present physical life. Edgar Cayce's insights provided him with the conviction that former lives play an important role in the "Journey to Oneness" of the soul as it seeks to become at one with its original Creator.

Let's now examine how our own past lives can be explored through a regimen of disciplined meditation and visualizations. In doing this we can unearth the depths of our unconscious memories, which have remained locked away from our conscious awareness.

5

REINCARNATION, PAST LIVES, AND KARMA

Cayce Meets Reincarnation

Edgar Cayce's first encounter with the idea of reincarnation startled, puzzled, and worried him. Cayce had completed many years of his astounding medical readings by 1923 when Arthur Lammers, a very successful businessman from Dayton, Ohio, approached him for a reading. At the time Cayce was living in Selma, Alabama, concentrating on the health problems of the many who wrote for help. Lammers was an intellectually curious man who wondered if Cayce's wisdom extended beyond the physical body and its ailments and into the realm of deep philosophical and religious beliefs and the ultimate destiny of the human race.

Cayce was intrigued. Perhaps these explorations might open up a new way to serve others, Cayce thought. After discussing this possibility with his wife, Gertrude, Cayce agreed to visit Lammers.

In a hotel room in Dayton, Cayce went into a trance to reply to Lammer's request for a horoscope reading. Astrology was one of Lammer's special interests. Instead of a horoscope, Cayce's voice came through with a blunt statement: "You were once a monk." Lammers excitedly told Cayce's secretary and a stenographer this could mean that Cayce might verify the centuries-old belief in reincarnation, with its implications about the continuity of life. Lammers went on with questions, one after the other.

Cayce was hesitant, but he agreed to answer them in the trance state that he usually used for medical readings. Astrology, Cayce felt, failed to take into account the many lifetimes involved in reincarnation. Cayce believed that the moon or planets caused the giant tides on earth to rise and fall, and had an effect on us all, but that it was questionable whether astrology could trace that effect with accuracy.

Over the following weeks and months Cayce continued to probe past lifetimes and their effect on present lives. He eventually requested that his secretary give him the sort of hypnotic suggestion she did for his medical readings, with specific instructions to his unconscious mind in its trance state. This marked the start of what were to be called Cayce's life readings.

Life Readings Begin

In the beginning Cayce had quite a struggle with the concept of reincarnation. His concern was reduced when Lammers pointed out to him that the Bible made several references to the subject. One passage in Revelation (13:10) suggested that a man who was born blind had been cruel to others in a past life and was paying for it.

Over the two decades that followed his encounter with Lammers, Cayce gave two thousand life readings and was surprised at the details that emerged. He named countries, dates, and activities of individuals in past lifetimes. These data were unmistakably confirmed in a large number of cases, eliminating coincidence as a rational explanation for their accuracy. Most of his subjects reported receiving valuable vocational guidance from these life readings, as well as guidance in improving relations with spouses, children, and others. These results encouraged Cayce to go on with his life readings as well as his medical readings.

The life readings emphasized that past lives were almost always responsible for a person's present character traits. Cayce emphatically stressed, however, that nothing could exert a more powerful influence on a person than that person's own free will.

Edgar Cayce taught us that our visit here on the planet is only one sojourn of many that go back through the ages. Each lifetime is our chance to learn and to correct the debit and credit balance of our lives. What we've done through all these sojourns is recorded in our subconscious minds—the residence of our never-ending soul. Our actions are also recorded in what has become known as the "Akashic records," which some call the "Book of Life." These memories are stored not only in our subconscious but in the Oversoul, the Collective Unconscious, or whatever we want to call it. Cayce claimed that all of his voluminous knowledge of his readings came from his ability to tune into these Akashic records.

Since the memories of our former lives and rebirths are not accessible to our own conscious mind, we have to try to unearth them by our psychic development. If we do, we might find some answers to our nagging questions and problems that seem inexplicable in our ordinary thinking.

A Better Life from Former Lives

Cayce pointed out that whatever our psyche discovers about former lives should be put to use to make ourselves better fathers, mothers, neighbors, friends. If we discover evidence of a past life in which we strayed widely from our harmony with the Creator, we should put that discovery to good use to shape a better life in the present incarnation. In this way we can learn from experience not only in this life but in many former ones and apply what we have learned to gaining a better spiritual understanding.

Cayce inspected closely the purposes for which we reenter this world from our former lives. Each of us in the present life has a physical, mental, and spiritual body. The spiritual part of us is everlasting. It consists of all that has happened during each of our sojourns here on earth. It is aware of our current physical attributes. It is also aware of our mental abilities. The spiritual self is also merged into the Universal Consciousness of God or the Creative Force—the First Cause.

The purpose of our spirit body being here in this sojourn, according to Cayce, is for us to be a co-worker with the First Cause. Our spirit body brings into our conscious mind an awareness of our mental, physical, and spiritual body. In this way each of us may know that we are part of the Whole and completely at one with the First Cause that brought us into being.

Cayce maintained that no soul perishes and that each is given the opportunities through many lives to make amends. He said that each soul enters into the physical plane for a lesson and for development. Of primary importance is our becoming aware of the Divine within. Cayce suggested that we become channels that allow the Creative Forces to manifest themselves in the material world. Each worldly experience then should be made into a steppingstone for the soul's final journey to its Maker.

Discovering Past-Life Clues

We have all had experiences when certain sounds, songs, fragrances, or flashes of insight bring us vague and ill-defined nostalgia and misty memories, which may lie buried in our former lives. We may discern clues of when or where they took place and thus contribute to our understanding of our present condition.

In September 1952, Hugh Lynn Cayce published a questionnaire designed to help individuals unearth possible clues to their past lives. His questions may elicit flashes of insight to help you understand your present life in view of past-life experiences. It is important to remember while answering these questions to use your intuition and not your analytical mind. Before you begin it is also important that you have been meditating regularly so that you are becoming more aware of your spiritual nature, where clues to your past lives are stored.

1. Describe any personal physical weakness that has persisted or recurred in your experiences.

2. How do you feel about this weakness?

3. Is one of your five senses keener than the others? Name it and give an example.

4. Is there any particular food or way of cooking food which you especially enjoy?

5. Are there any physical types of people that attract or repel you? Explain.

6. Do movies dealing with any particular type of physical activity appeal to you? Name one or more such movies.

7. Is there any type of physical activity you enjoy reading about? Name one or two books involving it.

8. What is your outstanding body skill or dexterity?

9. Note an outstanding physical fight in your experience. Did you win? Did you enjoy it?

10. What physical characteristics or traits do you remember about a person you disliked?

11. List the body habits you make a conscious effort to maintain.

12. What particular weakness or physical lack do you complain about most?

13. What body habits do you have that are unlike those of most people you know?

14. Is there any particular physical activity that you find especially exciting and stimulating, i.e., that you very much enjoy thinking about or participating in?

15. What physical ability do you wish for or do you strive to acquire?

16. Is there any particular physical injury or weakness you are afraid of having to face?

17. What physical weakness or handicap do you notice most in others?

18. Describe how you feel about people with the handicaps referred to in question 17.

19. When celebrating, do you seek food of a particular country? Describe by associating food with moods, if possible.

20. Do you enjoy cooking food in the open or like food cooked in the open?

21. Have you at any time:
    Liked long fingernails?
    Used a good deal of jewelry?
    Worn your hair in some special fashion? Describe.
    Attributed great sentimental or real value to some physical object?

22. Do you have a special interest in or dislike of any country? Explain.

23. Does this interest express itself in decorations in your home, interest in travel, or books you read? Describe and explain fully.

24. When you go to a museum, what section do you visit first, and where do you spend the most time?

25. Do you especially like or dislike any phase of church activity? Describe and explain—first experience, age, reaction, etc.

26. Is there any section of the country that has a strong appeal for you? Explain.

27. Have you ever read a historical novel about a country or group of people that strongly appealed to you? Describe briefly.

28. Do you remember seeing a movie about which you felt strongly? What was the subject of the movie?

29. Have you ever had a religious experience? Describe, giving age, nature of experience, etc.

30. What is your most absorbing hobby at present?

31. How much time do you spend on it weekly?

32. How many people do you know personally who have the same hobby?

33. How much time do you spend alone daily? Do you enjoy being alone?

34. Do you make an effort to be alone outdoors? Do you spend a great deal of time reading, or in libraries?

35. Do you have intense feelings of excitement or enjoyment concerning any type of group games or group activities? Explain.

36. Describe a problem that recurs frequently in your experience.

37. Is there some favorable condition or event that recurs? Describe briefly.

38. What faults do you notice most in others?

39. What weaknesses do you notice most in others?

40. Is there any type of person you are afraid of?

41. Is there any experience or activity you are afraid of? Explain.

42. What do you fear most?

43. What do you complain about most?

44. What type of music do you like most?

45. How much time per week do you spend listening to this music?

46. Do you remember any outstanding emotional experience in relation to music? What type was it? Describe, giving age, time, place, etc.

47. Describe a dream that you have had three or more times.

48. In your opinion, what is your outstanding talent?

49. List hobbies about which you have had strong feelings.

50. Have you ever suddenly been attracted to a person? Describe the person.

51. Describe one or more experiences which in your opinion indicate past lives.

52. Do you enjoy movies about any particular country? Name them.

53. Is there any type of circumstance or activity that you deliberately avoid? Describe.

The intention of this questionnaire is to explore the likelihood of reawakening your hidden memory to bring forth abilities, talents, skills, and impulses that could enrich your present life. Through answering these questions you may receive clues as to how your past lives directly influence your job, home life, talents, and relationships. Hugh Lynn Cayce believed that the clues could provide insight into your emotional reactions to the present.

One friend volunteered to answer this questionnaire. Since I didn't want her to have any preconceived notions of what these questions were supposed to elicit, I didn't reveal the nature of the questionnaire until after she completed it. The results were interesting. Ten out of her fifty-three answers related to India.

"I never gave a past life any thought," she told me. "But now I'm going to think this whole thing over—at least the answers concerning my strong attraction for anything and everything Indian, from art to music to food."

My friend went on to say that for Christmas her husband bought her two novels about India and she surprised him with an antique sitar, an Indian musical instrument, even though he doesn't play any musical instrument whatsoever!

"When my husband opened the gift he jokingly asked, 'Are you having an affair with an Indian?' "

My friend concluded that having lived in India in a former

life could possibly account for her overriding fear of poverty and her aggression in the work force in this lifetime. "My husband and kids are always telling me not to work so many hours, to take life easier," she said. "I honestly try. But when I'm not working I have recurring flashes of the poor people in Calcutta who live on the streets and beg for food. And I've never been to India! But I still have this underlying neurotic fear that if I don't keep working long hours we'll end up on the streets begging for food."

Exercises to Explore Former Lives

At this point let's review how we can probe for clues of past lifetimes. Scratching the subconscious mind for these clues is no easy job. The images that do float up are more ephemeral than those of forgotten dreams. But Cayce promised us that we will get images if we try.

Now that you've gone through this questionnaire, make yourself comfortable and get ready to review your likes and dislikes in quiet reverie. Breathe deeply as you do in meditation. Relax from head to toe. Try to lose yourself in your thoughts. Ask yourself what it is you would like to be doing, but have postponed. Perhaps it's studying a foreign language? Or visiting another country? Or maybe it's writing a book? Or taking up painting, sculpting, sewing, baking, gardening, or whatever.

Try to find a dozen or so items that appeal to you even if you have to reach deep in your mind for them. Now choose the one item that you feel the strongest about. Mentally picture yourself engaging in the hobby or using the skill you are concentrating on. Your activity may happen at any other time or place. Maybe you are painting a landscape in Provence or weaving a tapestry in Persia or fishing in Spain. Picture the setting with its sights, sounds, and smells. Let your free thoughts take you there.

You might picture yourself in a balloon. Imagine yourself in it as it soars in flight. Allow it to go wherever it will, unfettered. Remain relaxed with eyes closed as you picture your flight. Now visualize yourself as the balloon gently lands on the ground, softly and safely. What do you see? Where have you landed? Who are you?

Now picture a place where you can engage in your hobby or interest. Create a vivid image of yourself in this new setting. Have any other persons appeared to you? What sort of persons? What are they like? How are they dressed? What language are they speaking? Dwell on this scene in your mind's eye. What are your feelings about this scene? After about ten or fifteen minutes, find your balloon waiting to take you on a relaxed and pleasant trip back home.

The Cayce material suggests that you ask yourself several questions about your fantasy journey. What stood out most prominently in your mind? Was there a clue toward developing a new talent or interest? Something that stimulated you most? Can you apply this experience to your current life? Did the setting you encountered suggest a way to make your present setting or lifestyle more conducive to work? Did you discover an underlying purpose to apply to your present life to become more harmonious with people and nature?

We are often prodded by unconscious urges and impulses both from our early life here and in other lifetimes. The attempt to understand them can often bring us more contentment. If we repress these impulses without understanding them, we breed discontent. Cayce told us that one of the best ways to learn about our past lives is to examine our dreams.

When you dream, try to notice and remember small details

of background from architecture to scenery. It's extremely important to keep a notebook of your dreams because they are hard to recall. Usually only by tracing them in series does the logic emerge. The fragments have to be pieced together over a long period of time to give you either clues of past lives or insight into your present life. Some people have reported vivid dreams in exotic foreign locales that contain strong hints of past lives that explain current fears, abilities, and anxieties.

I recently came across a dramatic story written by Gladys McGarey, M.D., in the A.R.E. monthly magazine, *Venture Inward*. The article depicts the account of a past life that was revealed through a dream. Dr. McGarey wrote about a young expectant mother whose baby began to rotate into a breech position during the birth process. Fortunately, just before giving birth, the doctor was able to rotate the baby for a safe delivery. That incident was the beginning of a strange series of events that eventually led both Dr. McGarey and the new mother to believe that the newborn baby had lived before.

About a month after the baby was born, the mother began to complain to Dr. McGarey that for no apparent reason her baby would look terrified and then began to scream as if he were frightened. There was nothing the mother could do to calm her infant. One day out of exhaustion and confusion, the mother looked at her tiny baby and pleaded silently for insight into the cause of his fright and what she could do to help him.

That same night the mother dreamed that she was in the Superstition Mountains in Arizona standing next to the edge of a cliff watching a battle between pioneers and Indians on horses. Suddenly she saw one of the Indians fall over the edge of the mountain to his death. In her dream she went up to the Indian and as she looked at him he began to grow smaller and smaller until she finally recognized him as her own newborn son.

When the mother woke, she felt that the dream indicated that her baby had indeed been the Indian in a past life. She realized that her son may have been reliving the terror of falling head over heels off the cliff when he kept rotating his position before birth from head down to breech.

With this realization, the mother began to talk to her son each night as he was falling asleep. She would remind him that his past life was over and that he didn't have to go through that experience again. There would be no more terror in his new life. Shortly after his mother began those nightly suggestions, the baby became calm and happy.

Of course the exploration of past lives can sound pretty strange. But the fact is, such glimpses often happen and should be explored.

Many people traveling overseas visit a locale they feel strongly they have seen before. Specific streets, buildings, and landmarks are familiar. Some feel warmly at home in certain places.

This happened to me during a trip through Holland. John wrote about this in an afterword to one of my books

At one point it was necessary for us to meet a friend arriving by train at Hilversum, Holland, from Amsterdam. Hilversum is quite a large city, with a labyrinth of streets that must have been laid out by a herd of cattle. We were a little late driving into the city, and had no idea at all where the railroad station was. We found ourselves in a residential section of large homes, and there was no one around to ask directions. We finally found one lady wheeling a baby carriage, but she couldn't speak English, and time was getting tighter all the while.

Suddenly Elizabeth half-closed her eyes and said: "Go straight ahead. There's a traffic light about a mile and a half from here. The only traffic light."

If there was a traffic light there was no sign of it, even though this street was broad and stretched straight ahead. However, I kept driving.

"When you get to the light," Liz continued, "then make a right turn."

My hopes were fading, but I said, "Then what?"

Then she said, "Go exactly six-tenths of a mile. Six-tenths of a mile. Then make another right."

This was getting more ridiculous all the time. How could anyone judge a distance with that mathematical precision? But just about this point, I saw the traffic light looming ahead. That was at least encouraging. There were still no people around on the streets or sidewalks to ask.

We got to the traffic light, and I turned right, checking the speedometer as I did so. It was calibrated in miles, rather than kilometers, so I could check this ridiculous six-tenths of a mile. "What are we supposed to do after that?" I asked.

"We are to turn right again, as I told you," she said.

"Then what?" I asked.

"Drive for three blocks," Liz said, with her eyes still half-closed. "Then, ahead and on the right, you will see a rather tall building. On top of it, there is a large sign that reads GARAGE. The railroad station will be just in front of that building."

I knew we were wrong now. The word GARAGE didn't seem to be in common use in Holland—if at all. Poor Elizabeth had let her imagination run away with her. I looked at the speedometer, and it read exactly six-tenths of a mile from our traffic-light check point. On the right, there was a nondescript street. It looked almost as if we were on an alley or a dead-end street. I took it anyway, desperate now because of the lateness of the hour. There were trees on the road, and not much visible ahead.

But when we had gone two blocks, we could see clearly. There was a large building on the right. On top of it was a large sign reading GARAGE in two-foot-high letters. Just across the street from it was the railroad station. I was literally stunned. It was just about the first time Elizabeth had ever given me the right directions to anywhere.

At the time of that incident I never really considered the possibility that I had lived in Holland in a past life. In fact, I had no adequate explanation for how I just knew the area as if I had been born and raised there. Now, however, I recall that the month John and I spent in Holland was without doubt the highlight of our three-month stint in Europe. John was on assignment for *Reader's Digest*. On Saturdays and Sundays we used to rent bikes, picnic, and take endless walks along the winding canals as if we were locals. In fact, to this day every Sunday morning I go through the ritual of making a large Dutch pancake called a Pannekoek. Whenever we go out for breakfast my son will without fail order a Pannekoek as if it's a breakfast staple in this country.

I casually mentioned this to my mother, even though I know she does not believe in reincarnation. After long moments of silence on the other end of the telephone line she reminded me that when I was about seven or eight, a friend of the family brought me a pair of wooden clogs from Holland. The instant she said that, it all came back. The only time I took them off was for bed or bath.

Although clogs are not so popular today, I wear them as if they're part of my uniform. I even use them as house slippers—a fact that irritates John no end because they make so much noise. On several occasions he has threatened to run them through a wood chipper. In addition to John, my friends constantly taunt me about my un-chic clogs that went out of style in the late sixties.

Of course, all of these incidents are certainly not scientific proof that I was Dutch in a former life. But if I am to believe what Cayce said, then these incidents are signposts that point out hidden memories of a possible past life.

Past Life in Ireland?

One recent autumn day a friend of mine suggested I join her and another friend for lunch in the historically reconstructed seaport village of Mystic, Connecticut, about an hour-and-a-half drive from our homes. The atmosphere at Mystic is evocative of a New England seacoast whaling village. The shopkeepers dress in Colonial costume to recreate the feeling of life two hundred years ago.

We had barely sat down for lunch in a waterfront restaurant that overlooked the tall sailing ships of former days when I began to discover that our dining companion was delightfully obsessed with everything that had to do with Ireland. Although her last name implied different roots, her black hair, green eyes, and first name Maureen suggested Ireland.

Over lunch I learned she had been brought up in a Jewish neighborhood in Brooklyn where she found herself drawn toward Irish friends and teachers. At the age of twelve Maureen was taken along with her class to see the musical *Finian's Rainbow*. The following day, she painted a mural of an Irish landscape. From there her interest in Ireland grew. She began to read Irish poets and playwrights and constantly begged her mother to buy Irish records.

This obsession did not diminish with age. At fourteen she attended the High School of Performing Acts to pursue dance and the theater. On her first day of school she met a fellow student who combined both her Jewish roots and her Irish longings. He was half Irish and half Jewish. They married after high school.

As the years went on, Maureen's leanings toward things Irish took several concrete forms. Regularly she visited Jamestown, Rhode Island, where the landscape is reminiscent of the Irish coast. She dressed in Irish tweeds, listened to Irish music, and attended every Irish festival in town after she moved to Boston, where they are frequent events.

Today Maureen, with two grown children, is a psychotherapist in private practice. Every year she plans a trip to Ireland and for some reason backs away from it. "There is such a strong emotional feeling for the country, I don't know if I'm ready to face a visit," Maureen said as she sipped her bowl of New England clam chowder. "I can just look at pictures of Ireland and feel intense joy and sadness at the same time," she added.

"Do you know why?" I asked.

"I think it's because I feel the plight of the repressed Irish woman," Maureen said. "My closest friends are all Irish. Among them are two Irish nuns and a priest from Cork."

"Do they know about your longings for their country?" I asked.

"Very much so," Maureen replied. "In fact they keep encouraging me to go to Ireland."

I asked Maureen why she hesitated about going. Was it because she felt she had perhaps lived there in a former life?

"I just don't know if I'm ready to accept that I was Irish in a past life," Maureen said, "because I really don't know how I feel about reincarnation. However, I do know that this strong affinity I have for Ireland and Irish people has made me more effective as a therapist in helping my clients—who, incidentally, are mostly Irish. I feel as if we are somehow spiritually bonded."

I explained to Maureen that this is one of the main reasons Edgar Cayce believed we should recognize and acknowledge our former lives. The soul, Cayce told us, is the identity that comes down through our many sojourns. We are simply the sum total of all our experiences in every plane of consciousness.

"Can Cayce explain why this time around I chose Jewish parents?" Maureen asked. Her green eyes seemed to sparkle with a mixture of skepticism, curiosity, and belief.

Since karma is the law of cause and effect in action, I told Maureen that Cayce suggested that karma had drawn us to the parents we had chosen and to their resulting influence on us.

"That's interesting," Maureen said. Then she added, "I don't know if this means anything, but when I was born, my mother tells me that she looked into my eyes and spontaneously said, 'I'm going to call you Maureen.' That surprised everyone because traditionally Jewish parents *don't* give their children Irish names, especially with the Irish spelling."

"Perhaps your mother was responding to something deep in her unconscious—something inexplicable," I said.

Maureen took a long and thoughtful sip of tea and said, "So did I also choose to reenter earth? Or did my parents choose the time?"

"According to Cayce," I replied, "you yourself chose the time. Your Spiritual Forces viewed the opportunities and then you decided to reenter at the time of your birth."

"To learn a lesson?" she asked.

"Yes, and to grow spiritually," I answered.

"When you stop and think about reincarnation, perhaps it really isn't as far-out as it first appears," Maureen said.

"In what way?" I asked.

"Well, sometimes I'm counseling a client, usually always an Irish one, and I can actually feel myself take on the person's burden as if it were my own," she explained. "I often ask myself why I identify so intensely. I can never seem to come up with an answer," Maureen said. Then she hesitated for a moment, shrugged her shoulders, and said, "Maybe in a past life I wasn't compassionate and so I'm back to set it right."

I told Maureen that Cayce told us that awareness of what we're here to learn will enable us to develop further. He stated: "For what a body-mind, a soul-mind does about or with the knowledge or understanding that it has makes development for that soul" (476–1).

Suddenly Maureen turned the tables. "Liz," she said, "do you know what lesson you're here to learn?"

I told Maureen that meditation was helping me to gain patience and understanding. One of my other lessons was to overcome fear of heights. As a small child I would always get on the highest diving board trembling with fear. Sometimes I would jump. Most often I would climb back down. But there was something deep inside that always propelled me to climb back up until I lost that fear. Then at twenty-one I shocked my family and friends when I became a flight attendant. My brother said that the airline would have to equip their fleet with training wheels to get me on. For the first three months I was too frightened even to look out the window. Whenever a passenger would ask what we were flying over, I would go to the window, shut my eyes tightly, and guess. Usually I was so far off base that the passengers were relieved I was in the cabin and not the cockpit.

I went on to tell Maureen that after I conquered my fear of flying, I challenged myself to overcome my fear of mountains. I climbed in the Swiss Alps and eventually to the base camp of Mount Everest. All through this time I never understood why I was torturing myself to do things that frightened me so. It wasn't until I began to study the Cayce material on reincarnation that I realized that my unconscious, with its store of information on past lives, was prodding me to release myself from the burden of carrying fear around so that I could experience a greater sense of reality. Each venture helped me conquer fear and opened new doors—spiritually and materially.

I added that by going to the Himalayas, I experienced the automatic handwriting of the proverbs in a tent at fourteen thousand feet. Then there was the incredible experience of meeting Nima. He not only taught us about the Eastern world but saved my life on more than one occasion. Fortunately, John and I were able to return the favor when we brought him to this country for medical treatment.

"So you're saying that each one of us has a specific purpose for being here?" Maureen asked.

"According to Cayce," I said. Later I found the exact reading where he said just that: "For it is not purposeless that each soul enters an experience. . . . There are definite objects, definite conditions, definite experiences wherein they each then may be a help" (2054–2).

Maureen and I must have chatted for close to three hours. "Well," Maureen said as she slipped on her Irish tweed jacket, "I guess I had better head home. You've given me a lot to think about."

As we approached our cars, Maureen said spontaneously, "Next year I'm definitely going to Ireland! It suddenly occurred to me that by visiting Ireland, I'm not going backward. Instead I'll be able to look back, gain from that experience, and have a better idea of where I'm headed. I'll be gaining knowledge of the future.''

"Send me a postcard," I called from my car.

"You'll be *first* on my list!"

Skills from Past Lives

Cayce suggested that we should meditate on our own skills, abilities, and talents. These, he believed, have their roots in former lives and can bring us a cumulative power to put to use in our present lives. There's a fascinating case in the Cayce readings:

In 1934 Mrs. Mitchell Hastings requested a reading for her small daughter, Fredrica. In the reading, Edgar Cayce said that Fredrica would someday become involved in stained-glass artwork. The reading was all but forgotten until years later when Fredrica stumbled across it. She wrote to the A.R.E.:

"When mother died in 1946 we found amongst her papers the reading that were done of me in 1934. . . . Imagine my surprise to find the following in my reading:

'And there will come those periods when the activities in relation to art will deal with stained glass and activities in prism reactions' ''

Fredrica (now Mrs. Fields) went on to write: "Without knowing a thing at all about this prediction I was deep in the study of stained glass by 1946, with a deep inner feeling that this was to be my life. . . . ''

It had indeed become her life. Fredrica Field's work has been written up in such books as *The Complete Book of Creative Art, Decorating Glass,* and *Step-by-Step Stained Glass.* Windows that she had designed and executed appear in Greenwich, Connecticut, and the National Cathedral in Washington, D.C. In addition, she has been exhibited and won awards at the Corcoran Gallery of Art and the National Collection of Fine Arts at the Smithsonian Institution.

In response to Fredrica's letter to the A.R.E., Charles Thomas wrote: "I was fascinated by your letter and inspired by your stained-glass work. You are probably aware that we have a new library here. For several years, we have been searching for the appropriate design and an artist to do several small windows in stained glass for the Meditation Room. Might you be interested in a commission for such a set of windows?"

Fredrica wrote back, "It would be the greatest joy to create windows for the Meditation Room. I ask only that I may be allowed to do this as my gift to this wonderful project."

Today Fredrica's magnificent stained-glass windows are featured in the Meditation Room as a testimony to both Edgar Cayce's prophetic insight and Fredrica Field's talent and artistry, which, according to Cayce, have evolved over many lifetimes.

Probing Our Talents

Most of us do not recognize talents that lie buried in our subconscious waiting to be released. Cayce said that we must probe our talents and let them blossom. He was referring not only to our talents of this lifetime but of past lives from which there might be considerable accumulation stored in the hidden memory banks that we can draw on in the present.

A dramatic example of this is a case I recently came across in the book *Reincarnation* by Sylvia Cranston and

Carey Williams. In the book the authors write about a distinguished psychiatrist, Frederic F. Flach, M.D., who is associate clinical professor of psychiatry at Cornell University Medical College in New York. Cranston and Williams wrote that Dr. Flach first became interested in reincarnation while researching his psychiatric paper, "The Secret Strength of Depression." During this research he came across a 1620 treatise in Latin on the same subject. It was by a Swiss doctor with the same name as his: Friedericus F. Flach. His first impression was that this was a bizarre coincidence.

Dr. Flach, however, could not ignore the many similarities between himself and the doctor who lived four hundred years ago. The Swiss doctor was interested in depression, as he was. This was uncommon back in the 1600s. Dr. Flach found more parallels. They both originated from the same town called Flach. Both doctors had been married twice and each had three children.

Dr. Flach eventually went to Europe to retrace his predecessor's steps. He wanted to get a feeling of the area. In Basel he had a sense of warmth and of being home. Dr. Flach tells the story of his possible past life in his book *Friedericus*.

Childhood Memories

Think about some of your earliest experiences as a child. What did you most enjoy doing? Did you like to play certain games? Were they indoor or outdoor games? Were they physical or cerebral? Did you like to draw? If you did, what kinds of things did you draw. How about favorite stories? Were they contemporary or historical? Where did the stories take place? What about friends? Think about the main friendship of your childhood. Were there particular activities you enjoyed doing with certain friends?

Continue thinking about these memories for a few minutes. In childhood the memories of your former lives are bound to be most fresh. The Cayce material suggests that your leanings toward friends and activities are well worth examining for the clues we're looking for.

Let's experiment with an exercise that will help to evoke earliest memories of your childhood. Begin by making yourself comfortable. You may either sit or recline. Take in several long, deep breaths through your nose. After each breath, exhale slowly through your mouth as if you're blowing out a candle. Continue this deep breathing for five or so minutes, until you feel as if you have separated from your physical body.

Now you're going to transport yourself back to your childhood. Picture the house where you spent your earliest years. Wander through the various rooms, soaking in the sights, sounds, and scents as you do so. Perhaps you would like to mentally reach out and stroke the family pet, the curtain, the sofa, or whatever might help elicit concrete memories of your childhood. Perhaps you would like to stroll through the neighborhood? Pluck an apple from a neighbor's tree or a flower from your mother's garden? Visit your best friend or picture yourself and friends riding bikes, skating, swinging, or catching fireflies?

Now take yourself back a little bit further. Try to recall your first conscious memory. What is the mental picture you have of yourself? What are you wearing? What are you doing? Whom are you with? These images will probably be chaotic and kaleidoscopic. Don't let that stop you. You're about to take an even more daring step in your fantasy. But before you do so, keep your mind on several things: Remember Cayce's thoughts about the continuity of life? Life, as he defined it, is the conscious awareness of Existence. Your soul, Cayce said, has come down through many lifetimes in temporary visits to this physical world, with varied sojourns in different physical bodies. At the end of each physical lifetime we shed the body and enter into what we have called death. But death is simply passing through "the other door," to enter another cycle of the soul in an astral body or in another physical lifetime.

What it boils down to is this: Where were you before you were born into this lifetime? None of us can recall this consciously. But we can put our imagination to work. Think of it. Your consciousness must have been floating somewhere in this vast Universe before conception and your beginnings in your mother's womb. Being born here is parallel to dying from your previous life form. Birth here on earth, according to Cayce, is death from your previous existence. Conversely, death here in this present body is simply being born into another form of consciousness. In each cycle we are born into a learning process. We experience another form of "babyhood" in which our consciousness and self-awareness begin to grow. We have to start all over again.

Use your imagination to picture yourself at the moment you were being born into this physical lifetime. Imagine yourself as you actually were when you first blinked your unfocused eyes and became aware of the closeness, warmth, and love of your mother at whose breast you were fed and nurtured. Set in motion your creative fantasy. Remember, Cayce said that fantasy serves as a spark plug to bring the hidden reservoir of past events out from the unconscious. Fantasizing can be compared with putting the heat on under a kettle of water until the bubbles start rising and falling, some of which can be captured, as elusive as they are.

Using your fantasy, grasp that first actual memory you

can pull into your consciousness. Was it a soothing bath and a dry towel? Your mother's words of love and a smile as she drew you to her? A feeling of serenity and comfort?

Lose yourself in these memories. Feel yourself being wrapped snugly in a warm blanket. Hear your mother's heartbeat against your own. Reach out with your infant hands and explore her face. Explore your own face. Now ask yourself: What am I supposed to learn on this sojourn? Compassion? Love? Patience? Is there a particular skill I am here to develop? What were my skills in my former lifetime?

Open yourself up to receiving answers. Whatever comes into your mind reflect on it. But don't analyze it. Then meditate on the answers you have received. Most important, keep in mind that daily meditative sessions are imperative in all aspects of your psychic development, especially for unearthing past-life clues. And of course, don't forget that you may call on your spirit guides to help direct you toward achieving your goals in this lifetime.

The Word Within

In our search for clues to past lives, Cayce advised that we hear the voice within. Cayce was convinced that his knowledge, wisdom, and understanding came from reading of the Akashic records—the giant computer in the sky that holds every thought from the beginning of time. According to Cayce, every one of us is capable of reading these records. They are available for those who search within. In effect, we look within to find what is outside our limited scope. Cayce regarded the understanding of reincarnation as a vehicle for knowing the self. He summed up this idea by saying that we are what we are because of what we have been.

As mentioned earlier, one of the best ways to unearth who we were in past lives is through dream interpretation. Cayce told us that our subconscious stores memories of our past lives, both on earth and in the astral level. These memories weave themselves into the symbolism of our dreams. Of course, anyone who has ever tried to make casual sense out of their dreams knows how difficult, if not impossible, this can be. It's like entering a theater in the middle of a film, looking at it for only five minutes, and then trying to figure out the plot, characters, etc. Cayce realized this and offered step-by-step guidance in discerning what our dreams are trying to tell us. He believed that our dreams are given to us so that we may gain a deeper and more holistic understanding of ourselves. In turn, we will be guided to reaching our highest potential in our present lifetime.

At this point let's take everything we've learned so far in our journey to self-enlightenment and apply it to our next step—dream interpretation.

6

DREAMS

A Window to the Unconscious

Cayce believed that dreams provide us with a window to the unconscious and the soul. In other words, dreams are the way our unconscious talks to us. Cayce said that our dream analysis and interpretation were important in every phase of the psychic.

Dreams often "tell us the way it is" without censorship of the conscious mind, as Freud pointed out. Cayce said that consciousness is sought by man for his own diversion. In sleep the soul seeks the real activity of the self. He considered sleep that period when the soul takes stock of what it has acted upon.

Cayce believed that if we listened to our dreams, we could get important guidance in virtually every aspect of our lives, especially where critical events of precognition (an awareness of an incident before it actually happens) might be helpful to guide ourselves and others.

Foretelling the Future

Cayce said: "Any condition ever becoming a reality is first dreamed" (136–7). I found that to be true. One night I experienced a vivid precognitive dream that I'll never forget. John and I were in our hotel in Kathmandu the night before we were to start our trek to the base of Mount Everest. I woke up, literally screaming. I had dreamed our tent was being robbed out on the trail. The following day we began the trek. At sunset our Sherpas pitched camp for the night. We woke up the next morning to find that the base of the tent was slit cleanly with a native kukri knife. The camera case that contained our medical supplies and John's jeans with his wallet were stolen. Our Sherpas told us that we were lucky we didn't wake up. If we had, the robber would probably have slit our throats in addition to the tent.

I shuddered through the next forty days of the trek. To guard against another robbery, our Sherpas pitched our tent in the center of a circle of their tents. In retrospect I wish I had heeded the warning in that dream and had our tent pitched in that protective circle the first night.

Self-Understanding

Some dreams offer possibilities for better self-understanding, or for solving conflicts between our better and baser natures. An example of this is the following dream sent to Cayce. A man wrote that he and a fellow worker were in the smoking room of the stock exchange when suddenly the fellow worker began to make fun of his beliefs. "I replied to him roughly," wrote the man, "and told him some of his actions were far more disgusting than the peculiarity, seemingly, of my convictions. He became very sarcastic" (900–234).

This dream, according to Cayce, provided the opportunity for the dreamer to feel what it was like to receive the kind of treatment he had been dishing out to others. The dream was a direct channel for interpersonal communication, as many dreams are.

Health Dreams

Edgar Cayce believed that valuable information concerning the condition of our physical bodies comes from the unconscious mind. He said that most often these warnings come through our dreams. There are examples of these kinds of warnings throughout the Cayce readings. Charles Thomas recalled a fascinating dream that illustrated a health warning.

"Not long ago two women joined the A.R.E. because they shared an interest in dreams," Charles Thomas began. Their names are Val and Caroline. Both women believed Edgar Cayce's tenet that dreams are helpful in understanding what is going on in our lives and thought that regular discussion is a necessary step for interpreting them.

"They had met together regularly for quite some time when one day Caroline called Val and told her of a strange dream she had. Caroline dreamed that Val was sprinkling peanut dust over her five-year-old son's head. Val immediately felt that Caroline's dream was a health dream for her small son. It seems that Val had just begun the process of taking her son to an allergist because of a severe allergic reaction he had to certain foods. They were about to go through a very complex series of tests to find out what food groups he was allergic to. Several days earlier Val had expressed to Caroline how much she was dreading this tedious process.''

Charles Thomas continued to say that Val interpreted Caroline's dream to mean that her son was allergic to the peanut group. In fact, Val was so convinced of this that she persuaded the doctor to test him for the peanut group first. Reluctantly, the doctor did so. Sure enough, the boy was highly allergic to peanuts.

Dreams and Spiritual Guidance

Cayce believed that the most important and rewarding types of dreams are those that involve spiritual guidance. Here is an example of such a dream from Cayce's file (900–315).

''We were in a Palm Beach hotel, full of wealthy, influential people. I walked down the path with some who spoke and joked about women and I joined them. The [Spiritual] Master passed before me and out of the gate. I should have followed Him, I know, but instead [I] remained with these people, to whom I said: 'I don't know anyone here, but I used to. I used to chase around with Robert . . . ,' thus trying to make an impression on my friends about my previous influential companion.''

Cayce interpreted this dream as an important spiritual lesson. The dreamer lost the attunement with the Spiritual Master because he chose to cling to the physical, material world. He believed the proper response to a dream such as this should be hope rather than fear and anxiety. Dreams, Cayce said, can be a way of rediscovering the reality of God's presence in our daily lives.

Along with Edgar Cayce, Charles Thomas finds the dream of spiritual insight to be the most important. In this kind of dream, the interpretation is usually simple and obvious, with guidance for us to refocus our directions and commitments in our lives. Some people see religious figures or symbols in their dreams. Charles Thomas recalls a dream that his grandfather had.

For most of his life, Edgar Cayce and his family were plagued with financial problems—to the extent that it was uncertain where money for the next meal was coming from. The Great Seer struggled with his faith. He became depressed and frustrated because he could not provide adequately for his family. At such times, he gathered his family together and leaned on their encouragement to use his faith, to pray.

At a time of particular hardship, Edgar Cayce went into his study, read the Bible, as was his custom, and then lay down on his couch and took a nap, again as was his custom. He dreamed he was walking down a sidewalk in Paris with the duke and duchess of Windsor. This was not at all in character with the homespun Edgar Cayce. But as they walked, Edgar Cayce suggested that they stop and have a drink at a sidewalk cafe.

In his dream he was horrified with himself because he knew he had no money. He had no idea how he was going to pay for the drinks. To his further horror the duke and duchess accepted his offer. They sat down at a table as he wondered how in the world he was going to pay for his spontaneous generosity. They finished their drinks. The waiter brought the check. As the dream continued, Edgar reached in his pocket to pay. There was only one penny there. He pulled it out in his closed fist, and looked up at the waiter. There standing in front of him in the dream was the figure of Jesus, who looked down on the horrified dreamer. Then the image of Jesus laughed heartily and asked the dreaming Cayce, "Edgar, am I going to have to send you out for loaves and fishes?"

And that was the end of the dream. Edgar Cayce found no need for interpretation. He was reinspired and ready to commit himself to the work he needed to do in helping others tirelessly. His worries about the pressing financial problem disappeared. He was sure that the dream was a symbolic message from God that replenished his faith and enabled him to go on.

Telepathic Dreaming

Perhaps one of the most common types of psychic dream is one of telepathy—mind to mind communication. Cayce believed that we should be alert for possible psychic communication whenever we dream of someone we know. He added that the person we dream of does not necessarily have to be alive. It could be a deceased loved one.

A graphic example of this type of dream happened to my grandmother—the one who once told me that my discarnate grandfather communicates with her. She dreamed about a shoe box filled with silver dollars that my grandfather had collected over a lifetime. My grandmother said that my grandfather told her in a dream that he had hidden the box in our basement crawl space next to a "piece of twisted metal."

Of course nobody believed her. And certainly nobody in our family wanted to get on all fours and crawl into a three-foot-high space. Nobody except me, that is. Amazingly, just as my grandmother dreamed, I found a shoe box. It was coated with mildew and dust. It was also next to a broken fan, or as my grandfather told her in the dream, "a twisted piece of metal." Inside the shoe box were almost two hundred silver dollars, most more than a hundred years old. Later I had a coin from 1896 mounted onto a chain. I wear it often for good luck.

Dreams That Tap the Cosmic Consciousness

Cayce was convinced that valuable information from the Cosmic Forces or Universal Consciousness bubbles up to our consciousness through our dreams. He felt that this fact must be made known to the layman, scientist, mathematician, and historian. He claimed that any individual seeking higher information through these sources will find it to be true.

The famous German scientist Kekule found a dream of his that tapped the Cosmic Consciousness to be the source of a great discovery. He dreamed the exact configuration of the benzine molecule more than fifty years before its structure was confirmed by the scanning electron microscope.

There are dozens of other noted examples of information being channeled through the dreamer to benefit mankind. For example, there is the invention of the sewing machine: The concept of the hollow needle came through to Elias Howe in a dream. And Robert Louis Stevenson used his dreams to help choose the subject of his books.

Closer to home, I talked with friend and neighbor Stanley Mason, who is a prolific and successful inventor. He is responsible for inventing everything from the disposable contour diaper to Masonware for microwave ovens, the improved Band-Aid package, and the space-saving square milk carton.

"Every night for as long as I can remember," Stanley said, "before I go to sleep I give myself a problem to solve for the next day. Over the years my dreams have been as valuable as my waking state."

I told Stanley that Cayce spoke of this process as something that was not out of the ordinary, but a natural experience for unearthing information from our higher selves. Cayce said:"Dreams which are presented to the body are for the enlightenment of the consciousness"(3937–1).

Dreams and the Levels of the Mind

Mark Thurston, Ph.D., an astute Cayce scholar with the A.R.E., points out that to understand the meaning of our dreams we must understand the different levels of our minds: the conscious, the subconscious (or unconscious), and, as Cayce added, the Spiritual Superconscious. Cayce's theory was that the unconscious mind scans our memories and experiences, seeks a principle behind them, and projects them into our sleeping mind. As it does so, all the levels are interacting with one another, seeking to establish a meaningful relationship among themselves. And, as previously mentioned, there is the possibility that the subconscious mind of another individual will enter the picture to produce a telepathic dream.

This happened to me. Several days before my son was born, I had a vivid dream in which I was back at my parents' home and in my old bedroom. My mother was standing at the doorway holding a camera case. She told me that I had better pack a suitcase with the baby's clothes so that I would be prepared when it was time to go to the hospital. I was arguing that I didn't want to rush it. I had six more weeks before the baby was due. At that point my mother began to shove the baby clothes into the camera case. The next morning I got up and recalled the dream. It made such an impact that I actually packed the baby's suitcase along with my own. Later that day I phoned my mother to tell her of the dream. There was a moment of dead silence on the other end of the line. Then she told me that last night she had dreamed that at the last minute I left for the hospital without the baby's clothes. In her dream she was frantically searching through the attic for a suitcase. But she couldn't find one, nor could she find the baby's clothes. She said that she woke up grateful it was only a dream.

I thought this dream was interesting on two levels. It was not only clearly a telepathic dream but also prophetic in that we both sensed that the baby was coming a lot sooner that expected.

Dream Symbols

Cayce paralleled Freud when he referred to dream symbols. Cayce indicated that the consciousness of the soul is often influenced by the physical and mental experiences of the body. When such is the case, the physical reactions are often presented in the form of emblems. Cayce summed up a function of dreams by saying that in dreams, each individual soul reviews the experiences of its own activities.

Edgar Cayce gave some six hundred readings involving dreams. Many of these dreams were manifested to the individual in symbolic form. Cayce believed these symbols or emblems could be used for the benefit of the individual. Of course, in order for a dream to be beneficial, the proper interpretation of the symbols is critical. Unfortunately Cayce is no longer around to interpret our individual dreams. Even when he was, he emphasized that the best one to do the interpreting is the dreamer himself. No generalized book on dream interpretation can deliver a complete guide because no one other than the dreamer is familiar with the deep inner springs and memories. No one symbol means the same thing to everybody.

Although dream symbols are important in interpreting a dream, they are tough to understand. They emerge from deep within the subconscious mind rather than being images and impulses floating on the surface of the conscious mind. When we drop a hook to fish them up from the cloudy waters of the unconscious they may be so covered with mud and sand they are barely recognizable, even when cleared of the sediment. Still, the symbol may hold a clue for the growth of our awareness, and there may be multiple and complex meanings reflected in it.

Mark Thurston points out in his book *How to Interpret Your Dreams* that it is important to remember that the unconscious or subconscious mind is not simply a hidden version of the conscious mind. It operates on an entirely different level because it is tuned beyond ourselves to the Cosmic Universe. It speaks in a language outside the limits of our finite mind.

Dreams and Dying

According to the A.R.E., the most disturbing types of dreams people experience are those of death and dying. I was interested to learn that I was not alone on that score. I used to be an emotional wreck after waking from a dream in which someone close to me or I, myself, was dying or dead. Mark Thurston, however, put my mind to rest when he wrote, ''Most frequently the meaning of one's own death in a dream is the awakening of something new in the dreamer. Often this awakening is of a deeper understanding of the mind or spirit. That is, in order to come to a greater awareness of the inner life, one must let go of a merely physical notion of one's being.''

Thurston went on to say that if a person is physically

dying in a dream, the most likely interpretation is that a limited, physical concept of oneself is in the process of dying so that something new can be born.

If you're like I am, you might be somewhat unsure of how to discriminate between a symbolic dream (the dream of dying is symbolic of something new to be born) and a dream that is without symbols. An example of the latter is the telepathic dream I had of being robbed in the Himalayas. It was direct and to the point, not shrouded in symbolism. However, I recall waking from that dream and dismissing it as a symbol for my anxieties over the trek.

As you can see, confusion over what your dreams are trying to say can lead to a misinterpretation, which in turn can lead to major problems. This is where your psychic development enters into the picture. It is not enough merely to interpret your dreams on a conscious level. Your conscious self doesn't have all the answers. Very often the symbols of your dreams lay buried deep in the unconscious of this lifetime and past lifetimes. Our first step is to bring these symbols to the surface. There is no better way to accomplish this than through meditation. Meditation is the first step in stripping away the confusion. It is a direct pipeline to our true nature.

It is true that our dreams are a viable vehicle for transporting important information to us, but if we don't get the message, they are useless. Keeping a dream journal is, of course, important. But it is only a beginning. Attempting to decipher your dream journal in your conscious state can be like trying to bake a cake with only flour. You need all the ingredients to get results.

Cayce believed that the symbols that filter into our dreams are often fragments of our own personalities. They are usually something that the conscious mind has not yet grasped and are therefore clouded with ambiguity. The only way to try to understand dream symbols is to examine them in the context in which they have entered the dream. Consequently, the dreamer is the best qualified to find the proper meaning of the symbol. No one outside yourself can do it for you, although they can perhaps help you look for clues.

Of course, it's good to keep in mind why you want to try to unveil the mystery of these elusive symbols. Your most important purpose is to gain self-knowledge and self-understanding. The first step, as we will learn in detail, is to record and catalogue your dreams, especially if they occur in a series. Cayce suggested making an inventory and keeping the list to examine at frequent intervals. Recurrent symbols should receive the most attention. You should turn them over in your mind to examine what feelings they trigger and what they mean to you.

Mark Thurston defines a dream as having two features: the dream itself, with all the events and images it carries with it, and the response of the dreamer to that dream. The latter is the most important because the emotions evoked by the dream carry the personal importance that no one besides the dreamer can interpret except to suggest ways for the dreamer to reach for a meaning.

Ask yourself: What does this symbol remind me of? What are the feelings I get from it? What events in my life could have caused this symbol to arise? What action might it suggest I take?

One member of a dream study group I attended had a job that required constant travel. He came up with a list of symbols he frequently encountered in his dreams. He presented them not for the group members to interpret, but to get their suggestions about how he himself should interpret them. The list ran:

1. Continual train rides with vague destinations

2. Grand Central Station and confusion as to the proper track to find his train

3. Continual visits to elegant hotels

4. Continual visits to second-rate hotels

5. Chartering long series of large boats

6. Return to former jobs and work place

7. A remodeled house in the country

The dream study group was able to help draw out of him a strong negative reaction to all the items that had to do with travel. He finally got the courage to change jobs, at a financial loss. But eventually he became more successful than he had ever been.

Remembering Dreams

Edgar Cayce considered the dream world one of the safest and quickest approaches to the psychic world. But before we are able to interpret our dreams, we first have to set ourselves up so that we can remember them. Cayce gave four reasons why many of us may have a hard time remembering our dreams: lack of interest, physical exhaustion, impurities in the body (drugs, alcohol, or bad diet), and materialism.

The first step in remembering our dreams is, of course, to eliminate the above. Next we must instruct ourselves each night as we prepare to go to sleep: "I will remember my dreams." Repeat this phrase over and over. Drum it into your subconscious. Do it stubbornly, relentlessly, constantly. Our chances of dream recall without this are remote.

The Dream Notebook

Our next step is to have a dream notebook and pen ready beside our bed, where we can reach them easily. Also have a light, flashlight, or flashlight pen handy. Naturally you have to wake to make notes, but try to stay as drowsy as possible. If you don't wake during the night, make your notes first thing in the morning. Remember, you are delving into a third of your life that will otherwise go unnoticed.

Try to write the contents of the dream in as detailed a narrative as possible. But don't give up if you recall only a few shreds. Write those down even in the most scattered form, for they may contain valuable clues. Be a good reporter and answer the key questions of a journalist: Who, What, When, Where, How, and Why. Remember, if you don't get them all at first, pick up those shreds. What you are going for is a whole picture of continuity over weeks.

The Overall Pattern

Don't get too bogged down in your attempts at interpretation or you may feel overwhelmed. After you have a record in sequence of about a month of dreams you ought to have the beginnings of a pretty interesting novel-like story. It may be jumbled, of course, but you can now begin to put the pieces together and start to interpret the hints. Then you can sort out the symbols from the narrative. Soon you'll be able to see that the story line makes a lot more sense than that of a single dream. You may also discern a pattern welling up from that hidden unconscious.

Read, study, examine, and reflect on the symbols, the action, the people, the locations, and the events, allowing your waking unconscious to bubble up and help you interpret the meanings. And keep this rule in mind: You are the best one to interpret your own dreams. No one else can really do it for you. Nobody else knows the intricate interrelationships between you and your waking and dream world.

The dream is not only the open doorway to the unconscious, but to the soul and to the Universal Spiritual Forces. Cayce said that the purpose of all visions and dreams is to benefit the individual. When our dreams are correctly interpreted, they are the activities in the unseen world of our real selves.

It was Cayce's contention that we can steer dreams in a positive direction if we sincerely pray and meditate for a deep spiritual purpose in our lives. Our dreams will then be meaningful and helpful. If we don't pray and meditate for a spiritual purpose, our dreams remain scattered and distorted and fail to help us in our everyday living. This goes back to Cayce's underlying premise that our aim should be to get in tune with the Universe.

Solving Problems Through Dreams

Cayce believed that all facets of our being are revealed in dreams for the specific purpose of guiding us to higher, more balanced achievements in our mental, physical, and spiritual states. We may as well take advantage of our dreams to help us solve whatever problem we may be facing.

Before you go to sleep, think about your problem. Perhaps you're having a difficult situation at work, school, or home, or a troubled relationship with a spouse, friend, or lover. Or maybe you would like to receive creative inspiration. Whatever it is, it's important to remember that the nature of your question is vital. For example, asking how you can stop your spouse from drinking or smoking is not appropriate. It is not our responsibility to get another person to change. Instead, we should ask how we may receive better insight into ourselves: What is it within myself that allows such a situation? In this way we are programming ourselves to receive a deeper understanding of our true nature so that we may effectively deal with a troubled situation. This is not to say that we should not meditate and pray for others. That is different from trying to change them.

After you have thought about your problem for several minutes say either aloud or silently: "I am releasing this problem to my higher self. As I sleep I *will* receive an answer that will come through in my dreams." Now add: "I *will* remember my dreams." Once you have made those suggestions, forget about your problem. Believe that it will be answered through your dreams. Your answer may come over a period of nights or even weeks, or it may come in symbols in one night.

Group Enlightenment

Cayce recommended that we join with our family and friends to try to interpret our dreams and exchange ideas on them, gaining a fresh insight in doing so. Cayce said that by sharing your dreams you will gather a momentum beyond yourself. The A.R.E. groups report many incidents of group enlightenment in all phases of psychic development, including dreams.

A Dream-Sharing Experience

Let's take Cayce's advice and experiment with dream sharing. We'll begin with the usual group meditation. Carry on for fifteen minutes or so. Choose a volunteer to tell his or her most recent or most vivid dream. Remind the volunteer to tell his dream in complete detail, including the surroundings, characters, and feelings.

After he tells his dream, ask him to interpret it as best he can, explaining what the symbols or events mean to him. Now have the members of the group one by one pretend temporarily that they had this dream themselves. Individually they should begin to interpret the volunteer's dream according to their own lives as they begin to search within for their own meanings and symbols. In doing so, keep in mind that symbols mean different things to different people.

As each person interprets the volunteer's dream as his or her own, creative imagination may emerge to reveal formerly hidden meanings that could provide valuable guidance. In turn the volunteer, by listening to others interpret his dream as their own, will gather a more holistic interpretation of his dream. This process of sharing dreams with a group can act as a catalyst for greater self-revelation and insights that enhance psychic development.

The Fundamentals

Let's finish the process of dream interpretation by assuming that you've been keeping a dream journal for at least a few weeks. You have copiously recorded every shred of information that you can remember of your dreams. Perhaps you are starting to recognize certain symbols or recurrent themes, but are still somewhat puzzled. If so, stop trying to figure them out consciously. The more conscious effort you put in it, the more frustrated you are apt to become and the less likely you are to unearth correct interpretations. Instead of relying solely on your conscious selves, turn away from the physical, material world and consult the world within, where all information is stored.

It is important to keep in mind Cayce's fundamentals for achieving an altered state. You must have the highest purpose in mind. All fear, hostility, and anger must be replaced with love. Remember, every negative thought acts as a barricade to block your psychic channel.

With Cayce's ideals firmly fixed in your mind, sit away from all distractions. If you wish, turn on some soft music. Relax your body by doing the Cayce neck roll. Begin Cayce's meditation process to reach an altered state. As you start the deep breathing technique, ask your higher self to reveal what your dreams are telling you. After you have posed that question, clear your mind. Forget about your dream journal, symbols, and everything else. Focus on nothingness. Imagine your mind as a blank screen. Each time a thought comes into mind, wipe the screen clear. Don't become anxious for an immediate answer. Answers often come after meditation.

By combining meditation with keeping your dream journal, the missing jigsaw pieces will emerge, revealing a complete picture. You may discover direct confirmation that a departed loved one you dreamed about was indeed making contact, as my grandfather communicated with my grandmother about the missing shoe box with silver dollars. Or perhaps a spirit guide is trying to communicate through your dreams. Or maybe your dreams are providing insight into a latent talent. Or maybe a difficult problem is being solved.

The possibilities are limitless once you've mastered the technique of dream interpretation by tapping your psychic senses. But all this comes with practice and patience.

Another tool to help you interpret your dreams is automatic handwriting. After meditation is the best time to try this process. Remember to ask the specific question: "What are my dreams trying to tell me?" As your hand begins to write, it is important not to analyze or interrupt the flow until the session is over.

You are about to start on a great adventure. You are going to explore a world you've barely been aware of. You are going to embark on a mystery about yourself. When you've finished a month or two of your dream journal combined with regular meditations, you are going to read a detective story that will grip you. It will tell you things about yourself you never knew.

The tale will also be an adventure of travels you have taken to exotic places you never recalled visiting. Yet you have. Believe it. Your psychic insights will connect all the pieces together. You won't be stuck puzzling about an isolated, half-remembered dream. There will be a story about yourself you "never dreamed existed."

So make this project exciting. Don't forget that nightly command: " I will remember my dreams tonight." And get that notebook, pencil, and light ready beside your bed. At the end of a month, you'll be in for some interesting reading!

7

SPIRIT GUIDES

Increasing Cosmic Awareness

Edgar Cayce believed that each of us has a spirit guide or
guides available when we move into the psychic realm beyond the five senses. This type of entity stands by to help
as we reach into the Cosmic or Universal Sources. Cayce
indicated that they increase our awareness of the Divine.
He called them "Messengers of Truth," and felt that we
encounter angels without being aware that our spiritual development is increasing.

Growing up as a Catholic, I believed that without my
guardian angel (the Catholic version of a spirit guide), I
was doomed. I would never dream of leaving my house in
the morning without a quick prayer to my guardian angel.
In my childlike mind I envisioned my guardian angel looking
like Donna Reed with wings, halo, and flowing white gown.
As an adolescent, I updated her image a bit. I gave her a
dramatic bouffant pageboy hairdo, pinky rings, and an ankle
bracelet. But by the time I reached sixteen, got my driver's
license, occasional use of the family's 1960 Buick con-

vertible, and a few boyfriends, my guardian angel was put in dry dock along with my rosary beads, pearl-covered prayer book, holy card collection, and Blessed Virgin night-light that Aunt Betty had brought back from Atlantic City.

At twenty-eight, my spirit guides were back in the picture. This time, however, they didn't look like Donna Reed and they weren't Catholic either. This encounter with such enti-ties came as a result of an intensive psychic workshop I participated in. I recorded this experience in my diary to remind myself of the intensity of my feelings:

> *I never really believed that I could ever achieve a feeling that the Buddhists speak of as Nirvana, a mental state of perfect harmony. But I did. I seemed to lose all my earthly desires and passions. I had always felt that I was too much immersed in my own physical reality—my own ego—to experience anything mystical. It was as if I had climbed out of my body and blended with everything around me. I lost my individual aware-ness but gained something much greater. I suddenly became aware of a force that was so powerful it tran-scended all words. I felt as if I were being encompassed by thousands of white lights. But at the same time, brilliant colors were swirling everywhere. Then, there appeared a distinct sense of entities, or spirits. They were encasing me with love and protection. I felt totally at home. I didn't want to leave. I knew that I had to. But, I was also left with the feeling that I could return to these entities for insight, guidance, and truth. I just knew that all this was right.*

I had this encounter twelve years ago. Since that time these spirit guides have never let me down. The most dra-matic and poignant experience occurred when I saw them in my mind's eye and felt their protection when my son was born six weeks prematurely.

For a short time after Christopher's birth, his life was in danger because his lungs were underdeveloped. I sat for hours in the intensive care unit staring vacantly at my baby in the glass incubator. Tubes were coming out from his body in all directions. As I watched my baby's tiny chest rise and fall sporadically, I felt everything inside of me slipping away. I was frantic. While my entire family was saying the rosary, lighting candles, and making novenas to St. Theresa or whomever, I could only gaze at the small and fragile person I was afraid I would never hold. A Buddhist saying would occasionally flicker through my mind: All of our suffering is due to our strong worldly attachments to people and things. I knew that to be true. Nevertheless I had always been a clinger.

In an attempt to release myself from this misery, I began to meditate. I don't know how long I had been doing so when I suddenly felt the distinct presence of my spirit guides. I wish I had the words to describe the powerful feeling their protection and love brought. One moment I was an emotional wasteland. The next I was in some sort of protective bubble surrounded by millions of pulsating colorful lights that lifted me from the depths of despair into hope and contentment. My spiritual guides somehow made me understand that my power comes not from possessing, but from letting go.

During this meditation, I could hear the doctor and a nurse talking. Although they were physically only feet from me, they seemed light-years away. Up to this point, their every word about my son's condition sent quakes through my bones. But suddenly I realized that I had been using all my energy to run a silent series of images. I had put myself in the position of director, producer, actor, set designer, depleting all my energy trying to create a show I couldn't run anyway.

That same evening the pediatrician came to my room. He announced that he had some very good news. By morning Christopher's oxygen level would be normal. I should prepare his "going-home" suit for the following day. That night I went to sleep with a new reverence for the spiritual side of life. My spirit guides had become as real and necessary to me as a wise physician or a venerable counselor.

Spirit Guides
and Creative Assistance

Some impressive instances of spirit guides providing creative assistance have been landmarks in history. Take several cases that Mary Jo and Walter Uphoff have written about in their illuminating book *New Psychic Frontiers*. Chester Carlson, the inventor of the Xerox process, consistently carried out contacts with his spiritual guides on the "other side" and attributed his success in invention to them. He was so impressed that he bequeathed large sums of money to psychic research. Other brilliant minds who credit sources outside themselves include Coleridge, Yeats, Shelley, Tennyson, Beethoven, and Chopin.

Prominent psychic healers throughout history are quite explicit about the help they receive from their spiritual guides. One of the most dramatic and startling of these healers is the Brazilian known as Arigo. Unlike some alleged Philippine healers, Arigo became a "psychic surgeon" with hundreds of healings confirmed by several medical teams of highly qualified physicians and surgeons. Like Edgar Cayce, Arigo never went beyond grade school, yet he performed thousands of painless operations. He became known as the "Surgeon of the Rusty Knife" and his fame spread throughout the world.

Arigo insisted that he was guided by a spirit band. In addition, he said, his body and mind were taken over by a deceased German doctor named "Dr. Fritz." This phenomenon was so incredible that a team of American physicians were dumbfounded. Untutored Arigo spoke in German and wrote exact and correct prescriptions in that language at lightning speed.

The philosophical climate in Brazil was conducive to Arigo's beliefs. The country was dominated by the belief in Kardecism. To its advocates, help from the spiritual realm was constantly available. Kardecism was founded by a nineteenth-century French mystic who, along with his followers, believed in the reality of the spirit world. They became known as Intellectual Spiritists and have become so prominent in leading Brazilian medical circles that they have established two large hospitals associated with medical schools with over two thousand students taking four-year courses. They combine the study of traditional medicine with the practical use of mediums as an adjunct to orthodox medicine. Arigo's claim that he was aided by the mysterious Dr. Fritz and a band of spirit guides was taken seriously. Doctors at the largest hospital in Brazil meet often with mediums to review their patients, with confirmed benefits.

Another striking case of a spirit guide encounter involved a very down-to-earth British widow named Rosemary Brown. When she was only seven she saw a vision of a white-haired man who claimed that he would teach her music as she grew up. She recognized him from a portrait as Liszt. She claimed that he taught her to play the piano, dictating the movement of her hands. He then began instructing her to set down some four hundred classical piano compositions, entirely original. Some of these have been played by master contemporary musicians, including the London Philharmonic. The mastery and power of the music shocked critics. And no one yet has been able to explain the phenomenon. Rosemary herself claims that Liszt came through her to show that human beings are immortal.

Cayce told us that guardian angels come to us for creative expression. In reading 1646–1, he said, "The guardian angel . . . is the companion of each soul as it enters into the material experience—is ever an influence for the keeping of that attunement between the creative energies."

After I learned about Rosemary Brown, I sat down at our piano (never having played) and asked to be used as a channel for one of the Greats. I wasn't picky, Mozart would have been fine to start. Nothing happened. Not even bad "Chopsticks" filtered through. This reminded me that it's important not to expect earth-shattering experiences as proof of the existence of guides. Each one of us is unique. And each of us will bring our own unique experiences forth. If we expect dramatic displays, we will be setting ourselves up for disappointment and failure.

Cayce told us that our spirit guides are real and available whether we are aware of them or not. We just have to learn how to listen. One friend, a captain for Pan American Airways and student of Edgar Cayce, has learned how to listen to his guides as part of his daily regimen.

"Before I even get out of bed, I envision the 747 I'll be flying later in the day to be wrapped in a white light," the pilot told me. "I ask my guides to provide us with a safe trip. Believe it or not, ever since I've begun doing this things have been running a lot more smoothly."

"Will your guides just come to you?" I asked. "Or do you feel as if you have to call on them?"

"They won't impose on our own free will," he said. "Cayce made a point that our free will was more powerful than anything we have. But when we start asking our guides for help, their help can be greater than we could ever expect.''

"How do you go about calling on them?" I asked.

"First I meditate. Meditation, as you know, is for attunement—making contact with the Universal Source. After meditation and prayer I listen for guidance. As the Cayce material says, you ask your guides questions that can be answered with a yes or no. When I don't get a clear answer, I rephrase my question.''

"How do you know when you get your answer?" I asked.

"That comes with practice," he said. "It's different for everybody. I feel a certain vibration and know instantly that my guide is speaking to me. I talk to my guide by name.''

"Somebody you knew?" I asked.

"Yes, in a past life," he said. "I don't know if I have any from this life. But I do know that I have one primary one as my point of contact. I believe that at different periods of life we're assigned different guides.''

The captain went on to mention a dramatic incident that happened on one of his recent trips. "We were flying over the Soviet Union," he began, "when suddenly the flight attendant informed us that there was a passenger on board who was having an asthma attack and could barely breathe. We paged a doctor. The doctor administered a drug that the patient had with him. The doctor, however, couldn't determine the amount to give him, nor was he sure if an emergency landing was necessary. Hearing that, I went into the galley to collect my thoughts. I began to call on my spirit guide to help me make a decision if we should land. After a few moments I suddenly felt a calm come over me and the distinct feeling that the passenger was going to be okay. He could wait the one and half hours for our scheduled landing. I walked out of the galley and the doctor, who incidentally was an Indian, was applying acupuncture, and the passenger was breathing normally. To some I might sound as if my sneakers aren't laced all the way up. But nevertheless my guides have consistently provided me with help. Of course, the key to any of this is balance. Cayce told us throughout his readings to use all of our intelligence. That's what God gave us a good brain for. You can't go off the deep end, especially when you're hauling three hundred and fifty passengers through the skies. You use your analytical mind, and your guides are a bonus.''

Encountering Your Guides

Since Cayce believed that we all have spirit guides, let's turn to how you can encounter your own guides. Cayce told us they may appear spontaneously. In fact, you may be vaguely aware of them already since they are around whether you are in a psychic state or not. Our guides are considered to be a byproduct of both our conscious and unconscious states. Cayce believed that our spirit guides help us tune in to the Universal Consciousness, or the Christ Consciousness. With this in mind, we'll begin the first step toward meeting our guides.

The careful use of fantasy and imagination will help us to discover who our spirit guides are. It will also forward our psychic development while we escape the hectic pace of the modern world and seek the world within. We'll begin this process with Cayce's meditation technique for achieving a deep altered state. And remember that Cayce told us that the first lesson each of us must learn is that love is the giving out of that within self. Such a thought will help cancel hostility and negative thoughts. If you are experiencing any stress, it would be a good idea to preface the meditation with Cayce's gentle head roll or the exercise in which you tighten and then suddenly release all your muscles beginning with your toes and progressing on up.

Once you feel that you have reached an altered state of consciousness, imagine a peaceful and serene atmosphere. Perhaps it's a woodland glade carpeted with pine needles on a warm, tranquil day. Make the scene as vivid as you can. Then listen. Listen to a soft breeze blowing through the trees. Picture yourself looking down a shady trail along which your guides might appear. Perhaps you can create in your mind a relaxing sand dune by the ocean and an empty beach where your guides might be walking. Listen to the sound of the surf as it rolls peacefully along the shore.

Now mentally invite your spirit guides to come along the trail or along the beach. Ask them to join you. Frame in your mind the questions you would like to ask them. Perhaps you would like to ask them for direction in your life. Maybe you need help in making an important decision. Perhaps you have a family or financial problem. Or maybe there's a problem at work. Tell them your deepest secrets, being confident that they are there to help.

Cayce said that the experience of meeting your spirit guides is necessary for making yourself consciously aware of how your inner self may be controlled by such powers. We must be aware that we do encounter strangers that come into our consciousness. They reach to the inner self and to Cosmic spheres. And they come often. Greet them openly and with the spirit of truth. In this way you can encounter these experiences to increase your spiritual awareness.

After you have shared with your spirit guides whatever is on your mind, sink back in peaceful repose. Feel your body getting lighter and lighter. Feel it rise slowly as it becomes weightless. Don't look for an immediate answer. Instead, focus on the tranquility of the empty beach, or the

sound of the surf, or the woodland blanketed in pine needles
and wild flowers. Picture your spirit guides encompassing
you with their love and protection. Know that they will
steer you in the right direction and will be there for you
whenever you call on them.

Séance: Making Contact
with Departed Loved Ones

Another way spirit guides may manifest is through a séance.
In fact, one of the most powerful methods for exploring the
vast psychic realm is through a properly conducted séance.
Of course the word conjures up the image of a musty Vic-
torian mansion smack out of a Charles Addams cartoon. In
French, *séance* simply means a "meeting."

Although Cayce personally chose to contact the highest
source and thus had no need for a séance, he did acknowledge that a group can explore the psychic through a séance
when the group's combined energy is reaching the highest
goal. Repeatedly, Cayce was asked if it was wise to contact
those who have passed on. His typical response was that if
it was a helpful experience to each, then it was good. He
did warn, however, that selfish "hanging on" to departed
loved ones was not healthy.

When conjuring up discarnate entities, it is more important than ever to do so with the motive of helping others
either on this plane or in another dimension. We must harmonize with the Universal Consciousness under the protection of the White Light of the Creative Forces. Cayce
advised us that just because an entity has gone into another
plane of existence, he or she does not become all wise, and
is, in fact, not much different than when in the earth plane.
Each soul must move to its own spiritual development.

Sometimes well-meaning psychics have hindered that progress by keeping discarnate entities earthbound.

On the other hand, some séance groups have found that they can assist a troubled soul to go on to higher development by encouraging it to do so. As mentioned earlier, in the story of *The Ghost of Flight 401*, the pilots who were mediums conducted a séance—or "soul rescue"—to help their comrade move upward in his spiritual quest. There is a two-way street in spirit communication in which the more highly developed souls can bring comfort to those on the earth plane, or the selfless motive in the living can bring comfort in the other direction.

A dramatic incident of this "two-way street" in spirit communication happened during a recent séance at our home. The cast of characters "on this side" was John, myself, and our dinner guests, Anita and Frank Hall. Anita is a social worker and Frank is a Unitarian minister. Neither Anita nor Frank had ever been to a séance and were curious about the process. Frank, however, made it clear before the start of the séance that he would not be the best participant because he didn't really believe in communication with discarnates.

In his words: "Liz, I'm a Unitarian. We believe in helping only the living!" he said with an infectious chuckle.

Anita, petite and bouyant added, "Frank is religion's answer to Ralph Nader. Maybe with a little bit of Don Rickles thrown in."

"Speaking of Don Rickles," Frank interjected, "did you hear the one about Jack Benny, Bob Hope, and George Burns? When they finished playing eighteen holes, they went into their posh Beverly Hills club house, joined hands, and contacted the living."

After John shared a few too many of his favorite jokes, I explained to the Halls what to expect during a séance. I told them that in the scores of séances I have conducted over the years, I found that in many instances those who had never before had anything psychic happen suddenly discovered that they were natural channels for psychic communication.

Anita asked how that was possible. I thought one reason could be that they had simply never tried to be channels before. Perhaps they had been too involved in the physical side of life to bother to dip into the nonmaterial world. Hearing that, Frank told the story about the little boy who didn't say a word until he was five. Suddenly one day the kid says: "This oatmeal stinks!" The stunned mother asks, "Why have you waited so long to talk?" The kid looks up from his bowl and says, "Up until now the food's been okay."

I told Frank that that story was a good parallel. In order for a séance to work, there must be a need. I also told the Halls that each person in the séance circle can become a viable channel. No one should rely on the medium alone to come through with all the messages. If someone feels that he has received a message, he should verbalize it. Although the message may mean nothing to the person who received it, it may mean a lot to someone else in the circle. One friend, an advertising executive, discovered through a séance a number of years earlier that he was able to receive clear, confirmable messages. Another close friend, who is president of one of the largest real estate companies in the country, discovered that she had this same ability. I think the biggest misconception is that people who participate in séances by night are stringing pukka shells by day. Some of my most successful friends are natural channels. In fact, their natural psychic sensitivities may be exactly why they are so successful.

When I felt that the Halls had a good idea of what to

expect, I dimmed the lights—not in any attempt to make the place spooky, but to lessen the physical distractions. We sat in a circle, turned on the tape recorder, closed our eyes, and joined hands to tie the vibrations, creating a powerful psychic energy force. With our spines straight, allowing for a free flow of creative energies, we took five deep breaths through our noses with our mouths closed. We held each breath for the count of five and slowly exhaled through our mouths, feeling ourselves relaxing. We took five more deep breaths, breathing in love and exhaling all disharmony. Next we took in five more deep breaths. This time we imagined that with each breath we were becoming lighter and lighter and going higher and higher toward a spiritual white light. As we did so, we imagined taking our partners up with us. Finally we took three more breaths, sending love and energy down our right arms into the hand of the person sitting next to us. As conductor of the séance, I said softly that we would like to communicate with someone for only the best and highest purpose. If there was anyone who would like to come through, we were open channels. Then I repeated: "Only for the good."

Within moments I began to rub my legs vigorously. Since they didn't hurt, I knew that it was someone from the "other side" identifying himself or herself. This often happens. I asked who was here. Suddenly I received a clear mental image of an elderly man. He was wearing blue overalls and a plaid shirt and his two front teeth were crooked. I described this man just as I saw him in my mind's eye. Nobody in the circle said anything. I tried to dismiss this image, but it wouldn't go away. A few moments later, I strongly sensed that it was Frank's father.

"Frank," I asked, "is your father dead?"

"Yes," Frank said.

"Well, I think he's here," I said.

"Oh," Frank said. His tone told me I might as well have said William Shakespeare was here.

"The man I see is rubbing his legs," I said. "I feel as if it is his way of identifying himself."

When Frank didn't respond, I asked him if his father had had a problem with his legs.

"He had an embolism in his leg," Frank said. "That's what caused his death."

"And the crooked teeth?" I asked.

"They were so prominently crossed over they almost looked like one tooth," Frank said.

"Your father is saying: 'Remember the time I saved your life up on the roof?' " I said.

"Frank, that happened!" Anita blurted out.

"Oh yeah," Frank said, adding, "that did happen." His tone, however, had that same incredulous quality.

"He's saying that you and he were most alike. You were the peacemaker in the family," I said.

"Frank," Anita said, "that's what your father always said!"

"Yeah," Frank said thoughtfully. "He did always say that."

"Your father is now saying that you weren't like old hot head," I said. I asked Frank who that was.

"He's my brother," Frank said casually, as if flipping through a family album. "My dad always called him old hot head."

"Now I sense your father asking how Dotty or Dolly is." (I had no knowledge of the names in Frank's family whatsoever.)

"That's my mother, Dorothy," Frank said. He still sounded terribly offhand.

"The message," I said, "is that he is grateful that all you kids are looking out after her so well."

The image of his father continued to be vivid and the messages clear. "This guy's a real character," I said. "He's showing me how he used to keep nails tucked in the rim of his cap." Not having a clue what that was supposed to mean, I asked Frank.

Frank gave a rather unsettling chuckle and said, "My dad was a roofer. He used to keep nails in the rim of his cap."

"Your father's saying something about the 'old bomber,' " I said.

"That's what he called the family car when I was growing up," Frank mused. "In fact, my brother used to make my dad drop him off at the corner of the schoolyard so that none of his friends would see him getting out of the 'old bomber.' "

We all laughed. But suddenly the mood shifted. "Frank," I said, "your father is saying, 'Remember shortly after I died, you were in your car and you felt my presence and began talking to me? I want you to know that I am always with you.' "

With those words, the image of Frank's father faded. We closed the séance by visualizing the entity going back to the spiritual white light. Then we took several deep breaths, once again breathing in love and exhaling peace and harmony.

Messages Confirmed

Over chocolate mousse cake and coffee Frank told us that the only time he had ever felt his father's presence was while in his car driving home from New York. Frank said that his father's presence had been so strong that he had, as the message said, spoken out loud to him. Afterwards he felt foolish for talking to someone who wasn't there. He had never told anyone about the incident—not even Anita.

The next day, Frank and Anita left Westport to spend the summer at their cabin in Maine. A week later I received a letter from Frank.

Dear Liz,

I've been thinking about our séance and your "meeting" with my father. You know how skeptical I was, so you must know how unsettling it was for me to realize that he—or his "spirit" or whatever—was coming through.

I didn't say much during the séance. One reason for my untypical reserve was that I didn't want to lead you by saying things that would suggest what you might think or say. Another reason for my limited verbal response was that my mind was going a mile a minute, racing back and forth between my usual skepticism and the incredible possibility that there was some real, unexplainable communication happening. I guess I dragged my feet along that path, but once I was there it was most convincing.

Now that I'm relaxing at the ocean I find myself rationalizing the experience away. But I can't dismiss it so easily. When you were describing my father and relaying the messages coming from him, I was fully convinced and felt his presence. Somehow I stopped doubting and questioning long enough to "let it happen."

Today I came across a line from an F. Scott Fitzgerald novel, and, in part at least, it prompted me to write to you. He said: "The test of a first-rate intelligence is the ability to hold two opposed ideas in the mind at the same time, and still retain the ability to function.''

I don't claim a first-rate intelligence, but I do hold those two opposing ideas—that my father ''came through,'' and he couldn't possibly have done so!

Maybe those two opposites will provide a creative tension, like the ends of a violin string, and I'll hear more music!

See you soon. (Shall we bring back some lobster from Maine?)

Cheers,
Frank

Before we turn to how you can go about experimenting with your own séance, let me remind you of the importance of offering help to a possibly troubled spirit entity. Fortunately Frank's father did not appear troubled. On the other hand, Don Repo, the flight engineer on flight 401, was a troubled spirit. He wanted desperately to clear the name of flight 401 and he wanted his wife, Alice, to know that he loved her and was still with her. The strong messages that John and I received telling us to contact his widow set up quite a dilemma for us. Neither of us could figure a graceful way to phone his grieving widow and tell her that we had been in apparent communication with her dead husband. However, when the messages from Don showed no sign of letting up, John decided to write to Don's daughter, Donna, a flight attendant. Since we didn't have Donna's address, John sent the letter in care of her mother.

A week later Donna phoned. She told John that something very strange had just happened. She had just returned from a trip. Her mother dropped by to visit and brought along John's letter. After her mother left, Donna read the letter.

She was about to rip it up, when the phone rang. It was her mother. She asked Donna what the name in the return address on the envelope was. Donna told her that it was John G. Fuller. Her mother said that all the way home she had been trying to figure out why that name sounded so familiar. When she got back home she suddenly realized why. A friend of hers had recently dropped off one of John's books for her to read. Alice had stayed up half the night reading it. Alice told Donna the book was so absorbing, that in spite of their policy not to talk to journalists writing about flight 401, she wanted to meet us.

During our subsequent visit, Alice confided: "One night I was sleeping and smelled this very strong odor of Vitalis on the pillow," she said. "That was what Don used on his hair. He used it for years and years. I was sleeping, and that smell actually woke me up. At first I thought maybe it was coming from a pillowcase I hadn't used for a long time. But I had bought all new pillows and pillowcases. So there couldn't have been any tonic on them.

"Then another time," Alice continued, "I just felt that he was right there in bed with me. It wasn't a dream. I was just so aware that he was there. I said, 'I don't believe it. It can't be you.' I said, 'Let me feel your hands.' I felt his wedding band. I could feel the dent he had in his ring. I said, 'I know it's you.' Yet, I was skeptical. I thought this can't be."

Prior to talking to Alice Repo, I had received very detailed information psychically. The information involved minutiae that if confirmed would be very strong evidence that Don's consciousness had survived his death.

The psychic messages from Don Repo included:

The intimate name he always called Alice (Sassy)
The barrel of pennies Don collected

The fact that they had "mice in the family room closet"
The brand name of his favorite beer

Each of these bits and pieces checked out exactly: Sassy
had been Alice's nickname for years. After Don died, the
barrel of pennies he had collected was moved into his son's
room. Just weeks earlier they had set traps to get rid of the
mice in what they called "the family room closet." And in
the kitchen cupboard were Meister Brau mugs—the only
brand of beer Don would drink.

These messages brought great comfort to Alice Repo.
They also presented undeniable evidence that the end of life
on earth indeed was simply going through "God's other
door."

A properly conducted séance can comfort the living as
well as departed loved ones. With this in mind, we can
proceed with the steps necessary for you to experiment with
your own séance.

Conducting Your Own Séance

Invite a group of friends, whether psychic or not, to your
home for a session. If you like, you may serve them coffee
or tea. Alcohol is definitely a hindrance. It is best if some
of your friends actively want to communicate with specific
discarnate spirits, and if those spirits had been creative and
positive persons while on the earth plane.

Begin the séance by sitting in a circle. Four to six people
is an optimal number, not too many to produce confusing
signals. Lights should be dimmed to reduce distractions,
but darkness is not recommended. All participants should
hold hands. This combines the energies and provides a com-
monality of purpose.

You as leader should open the session with a preamble. For example: "We have gathered here with the highest purpose, to reach for and communicate with those we have loved in life and to whom we want to bring the highest spiritual inspiration, and from whom we want to receive the same."

Now instruct the group in the deep breathing process I used in the séance I had with the Halls. Let's review that: With straight spine, take five deep breaths through the nose with mouth closed. Hold each breath for the count of five. Slowly exhale through the mouth, feeling yourself relax. Take in five more deep breaths, breathing in love and exhaling all disharmony. Now take in five more deep breaths. Imagine that with each breath you are becoming lighter and lighter and going higher and higher toward a spiritual white light. As you lift, take your partners with you. Feel the group energy as you soar. Finally, take three more breaths, sending love and energy down your right arm and into the hand of the person sitting next to you. Receive the energy through your left hand and send it out your right hand.

Now you may ask someone in the group to speak up and call whatever entity he or she wants to contact for the highest purpose. You may also ask for Creative Forces of the Universe to join in and assist this meeting. Once you have done so, ask for the pure white light of these forces to surround the group and protect it.

After this, be still, be giving, and be humble. Cayce told us that the individual who loses self for others may develop the greater expression of psychic forces.

It is important to verbalize whatever images suddenly come into your mind. Remember, your thoughts and images may mean nothing to you, but may mean something to someone else in the circle. For instance, had I not revealed the images I received of Frank's father, Frank would never have had communication that was critical in verifying the reality of spirit communication. It's also important for everyone in the circle, developed psychic or not, to describe in detail what they are receiving, as strange as it may sound.

If the energy begins to fade, the name of the entity may be repeated and those on the ground should send love and energy. Each participant should say mentally, "We wish to communicate with _____ at this time. If it is possible, please use us as channels."

After twenty to thirty minutes, release the entity. In closing the séance, each person should visualize the entity returning to the spiritual white light.*

Let's look at other facets of the psychic that can offer further clues to some of the mysteries beyond the five senses. One of the most fascinating of these is the human aura. Edgar Cayce's aura interpretation can provide illuminating insights into ourselves and others, and these insights can increase our psychic awareness to make our life as productive and meaningful as possible.

---

*The Edgar Cayce readings suggest caution in exploring this area. I, however, have found this technique helpful.

AURAS, COLORS, AND ASTROLOGY

What Are Auras?

An aura is simply the outward reflection of the vital energies within an individual. The aura reveals a person's spiritual and physical condition. Normally this energy extends outward from the physical body and can most easily be seen around the head and shoulder area, although it surrounds the entire body. According to Cayce, the majority of us see auras surrounding others, but fail to realize it.

"Ever since I can remember I have seen colors in connection with people," Edgar Cayce wrote in his book entitled *Auras*. "I do not remember a time when the human beings I encountered did not register on my retina with blues and greens and reds gently pouring from their heads and shoulders. It was a long time before I realized that other people did not see these colors; it was a long time before I heard the word aura, and learned to apply it to this phenomenon which to me was commonplace.

"I do not ever think of people except in connection with their auras," Cayce continued. "I see them change in my friends and loved ones as time goes by—sickness, dejection, love, fulfillment—these are all reflected in the aura, and for me the aura is the weathervane of the soul. It shows which way the winds of destiny are blowing.''

Auras and History

The notion that we all have an energy field was not new with Cayce. In 500 B.C. Pythagoras wrote about a light radiating from humans that was said to be responsible for creating a variety of physical effects. Twelfth-century scholars postulated that one person can affect another simply by the presence of the energy emanating from his body. Today extensive research on the energy field surrounding the human body is being conducted in leading universities. Recently the Energy Research Group in New York City developed a method of viewing the human aura on video tape. This group of scientists report that, ''A thin pulsating field was displayed around the human body.''

Dr. Harold Burr at Yale University says that the idea of the aura does not seem far-fetched to him. He believes that since we know that the ranges of perception in individual sight, hearing, smell, etc., vary greatly, we cannot summarily say that because we have not experienced it, it does not exist.

A Healthy Aura

Roberta Tager, a spiritual health therapist in Westport, Connecticut, believes that through the energy field people can heal themselves. ''When a person is in a negative frame of mind, due to fear or anger or whatever, his aura will be shrunken inward,'' Roberta says. "If he remains in this condition for a prolonged length of time, imbalance manifests with the physical body. This is a sign to the individual that something has gone wrong in his thinking and usually requires an attitudinal change to readjust the energy and reconstruct a healthy aura.

"For instance, did you ever find that you're immediately repelled by a person for no apparent reason?'' Roberta asks. "Well there is a reason. Your energies have clashed to create negative feelings. You can, however, overcome negative energy by sending positive thoughts. A thought that is soft and gentle is actually nourishing a person's highest self through their aura field.

"The best thing you can do when you encounter negative energy is to send positive energy. If you react in the same negative way, what you're doing is fueling the negative engines.''

Seeing with More Than Your Eyes

The most vivid aura I have ever seen was around the head of the famous Dutch clairvoyant, Gerard Croiset. John and I had once spent a month observing Croiset's extraordinary psychic powers for an article John was writing for *Reader's Digest*. Croiset would conduct multiple healing sessions at one moment and the next would be on the phone helping police from all over the world locate missing people. Croiset, like Cayce, used his powers for only the highest and most constructive of purposes. In fact, one day during our visit, a woman called and wanted help finding her misplaced false teeth. Croiset hung up on her.

The aura I saw over Croiset appeared during a healing session in his typically Dutch home near a scenic canal. I watched Croiset cup his hands around an elderly man's head. Croiset's eyes were closed and from his intense expression I assumed he was in a deep, deep concentration. Suddenly there appeared a bright glow emanating from Croiset's bushy red hair. I turned to John to see if he could see the same thing, but when I looked back the aura was gone. I believed that it was probably still there but that I had become so distracted explaining the aura to John that I was in no frame of mind to see it again.

That evening Croiset took us to his son's new restaurant, a rustic and charming inn. Over dinner I mentioned the aura I had seen over his head. Croiset broke into his ebullient laugh and said, "Good, you're learning to see with more than your eyes! That's a very valuable asset."

Measuring the Aura

Professor W. H. C. Tenhaeff, director of parapsychology at the University of Utrecht in Holland, conducted laboratory experiments on Croiset to demonstrate a flow of energy emanating from Croiset as he healed. In 1939 Edgar Cayce predicted that this would happen one day. He said that when scientists give spiritual phenomena the same attention they have given material phenomena, the human aura will become as measurable as any other aspect of human experience.

Cayce's prediction seems to have been on target. One of the most important scientific breakthroughs in determining the validity of auras has come with Kirlian photography, developed by Soviet scientists. An electromagnetic halo projecting from the human body and other life forms can be seen on infrared film. Kirlian research suggests that the aura is brighter and larger when a person is in meditation or prayer.

This helps explain the halo I saw around Gerard Croiset. He could be said to have been in deep meditation. This could also explain why saints and other spiritual figures are depicted with light around their bodies. Perhaps they are emitting a light due to their intense concentration of spiritual force. Artists thousands of years ago and thousands of miles apart all use the symbol of the halo to indicate spirituality—in Islamic, Greek, Buddhist, and Christian art.

"An aura is an effect, not a cause," Edgar Cayce continued in his book. "Every atom, every molecule . . . tells the story of itself, its pattern, its purpose, through the vibrations which emanate from it. Colors are the perceptions of these vibrations by the human eye. As the souls of individuals travel through the realms of being they shift and change their patterns as they use or abuse opportunities presented to them. Thus at any time . . . a soul will give off through vibrations the story of itself and the condition in which it now exists . . . So, when I see an aura, I see the man as he is . . . By experience I have learned to tell a good deal from the intensity of colors."

The Meaning of the Colors

Cayce told an anecdote about how on first meeting a particular man, he had seen a shaft of light coming downward over the man's left shoulder. In the shaft of light, Cayce saw white, plus a great deal of green and red with blue mixed in it. Cayce interpreted this as a sign that the man was receiving inspiration and was using it for constructive purposes.

"I wondered if he was a writer," Edgar Cayce wrote, "for it struck me that this would be a proper aura for such work. I asked him, and he told me that although he had been a writer, he was now engaged in lecturing and teaching, still giving information for the help of others.''

In another example Cayce read the aura of a middle-aged schoolteacher: ''There is a great deal of leaden gray in your aura,'' Cayce dictated about the subject, ''not only from your physical condition but because you have been doubting your own beliefs. You have become fearful of the thing to which you have entrusted your whole inner self. There also rise some smears of white, coming from your higher intellectual self, and from your spiritual intents and purposes. Broaden these. You also have a great deal of indigo, indicating spiritual seeking. There is green, but often fringed with red, for sometimes you would like to be in the other fellow's place, and would like him to be in your place, so that he'd know what you go through.''

A further example is Cayce's aura reading for a young nurse: ''In your aura there is a great deal of green, but you often rub it out with blue, then streak it up with red. I would not want to be around when you do the streaking, and most people who know you feel the same way, for when you let go it is quite a display of temper. You have a good deal of ability, especially in being able to act as a healing and helpful influence to others. Consequently, the principal color in your aura is green, but you streak it up when you desire to have your own way.''

And still a further example is a reading for a secretary: ''There has been a great deal of red about you lately, which means that you have been rather defiant. Often I have seen lines running away from your fingers when I can't see the aura about your face. That is probably because you think with your fingers, writing so much. In the last few days you have had a great deal of purple, which means the spiritual has mingled with your defiance; your desire and hope for better things has influenced your doubts and fears. You are sure, but a little fearful at times that you will not be able to put it over. You also have a great deal of coral and pink, meaning activity, but at times you smear it with more green than white, which indicates your desire to help others irrespective of themselves. That is not God's way.''

Cayce offered these examples in his book to show how colors blend to form an aura and how they change according to the situation. He believed that we could all begin to learn to read auras by becoming conscious of the colors of the clothes people wear, the dominant colors in their homes, the flowers they choose for their gardens and even in their pets. "It can be a fascinating game," Cayce wrote, "noticing how any person with vitality and vigor will have a little splash of red in a costume, in a room, or in a garden; noticing how persons who are quiet, dependable, sure of themselves, and spiritual, never are seen without deep blues—it is almost as if they turn things blue by being near them. Notice how bright and sunny people, who like to laugh and play, and who are never tired or downhearted, will wear golden yellow and seem to color things yellow, like a buttercup held under the chin.''

The Perfect Aura

Speaking generally about colors, Cayce said in his book that colors influence the individual a great deal more than even musical tones. He said that drabs or certain greens have an effect that may actually bring illness to the physical body. On the other hand, purples, violets, or shades of tan bring an exultant affect.

Edgar Cayce's Color Chart

Here is Edgar Cayce's color chart:

COLOR	INTERPRETATION	AFFLICTION
Red	Force, vigor, energy	Nervousness, egotism
Orange	Thoughtfulness, Consideration	Laziness, repression
Yellow	Health, well-being, friendliness	Timidity, weakness of will
Green	Healing, helpful	Mixed with yellow—deceit
Blue	Spiritual, artistic, selfless	Struggle, melancholy
Indigo	Seeking, religious	Heart and stomach trouble
Violet	Seeking, religious	Heart and stomach trouble

The following is Edgar Cayce's interpretation of the color chart:

RED

"As to the meaning of red, it indicates force, vigor and energy. Its interpretation depends upon the shade, and as with all colors, upon the relationship of other colors. Dark red indicates high temper, and it is a symbol of nervous turmoil. A person with dark red in his aura may not be weak outwardly, but he is suffering in some way, and it is reflected in his nervous system. Such a person is apt to be domineering and quick to act. If the shade of red is light, it indicates a nervous, impulsive, very active person, one who is probably self-centered. Scarlet indicates an overdose of ego. Pink or coral is the color of immaturity. It is seen usually in young people, and if it shows up in the aura of one who is grown, it indicates delayed adolescence, a childish concern with self. In all cases of red there is a tendency to nervous troubles, and such people ought to take time to be quiet and to get outside themselves."

ORANGE

"Orange is the color of the sun. It is vital, and a good color generally, indicating thoughtfulness and consideration of others. Again, however, it is a matter of shade. Golden orange is vital and indicates self-control, whereas brownish orange shows a lack of ambition and a don't-care attitude. Such people may be repressed, but usually they are just lazy. People with orange in their auras are subject to kidney trouble."

YELLOW

"When it is golden yellow it indicates health and well-being. Such people take good care of themselves, don't worry, and learn easily; good mentality is natural in them. They are happy, friendly, and helpful. If the yellow is ruddy, they are timid. If they are redheads they are apt to have an inferiority complex. They are thus apt often to be indecisive and weak in will, inclined to let others lead them."

GREEN

"Pure emerald green, particularly if it has a dash of blue, is the color of healing. It is helpful, strong, friendly. It is the color of doctors and nurses, who invariably have a lot of it in their auras. However, it is seldom a dominating color, usually being overshadowed by one of its neighbors. As it tends toward blue it is more helpful and trustworthy. As it tends toward yellow it is weakened. A lemony green, with a lot of yellow, is deceitful. As a rule the deep, healing green is seen in small amounts, but it is good to have a little of it in your aura."

BLUE

"Almost any kind of blue is good, but the deeper shades are the best. Pale blue indicates little depth, but a struggle toward maturity. The person may not be talented, but he tries. He will have many heartaches and many headaches, but he will keep going in the right direction. The middle blue, or aqua, belongs to a person who will work harder and get more done than the fellow with light blue, though there may be little difference between them in talent. Those with the deep blue have found their work and are immersed in it. They are apt to be moody and are almost always unusual persons, but they have a mission and they steadfastly go about fulfilling it. They are spiritual-minded for the most part, and their life is usually dedicated to an unselfish cause, such as science, art, or social service. I have seen many Sisters of Mercy with this dark blue, and many writers and singers also."

INDIGO AND VIOLET

"Indigo and violet indicate seekers of all types, people who are searching for a cause or a religious experience. As these people get settled in their careers and in their beliefs, however, these colors usually settle back into deep blue. It seems that once the purpose is set in the right direction, blue is a natural emanation of the soul. Those who have purple are inclined to be overbearing, for here there is an infiltration of pink. Heart trouble and stomach trouble are rather commonplace in persons with indigo, violet, and purple in their auras."

WHITE

"The perfect color, of course, is white, and this is what we all are striving for. If our souls were in perfect balance, then all our color vibrations would blend and we would have an aura of pure white. Christ had this aura . . ."

Healing Properties in Colors

The works of Cayce indicate certain healing properties in colors. He said that the spiritual body responds to color forces as it does to medicine. Cayce considered natural light as the most life-giving and the best and most logical reflection of the creative forces. He seemed to sense a palpable effect of color, since color is vibration, and vibration is the essence of all life and energy. Our color selection in clothes and surroundings thus has a profound effect on our psyche and that of others.

Shape of the Aura

In addition to colors, Cayce said that the shape of the aura is often a helpful indicator of temperament. "In the green aura of healers," he wrote, "if the color quivers as it rises, the person is most sympathetic. Several times I have seen people in whose auras there were little hooks of light here and there. In each case the man had a job as overseer of large groups of other men, a director and a leader."

Cayce went on to write that the shape of a child's aura can also reveal temperament. "If the child is reasonable and will accept instruction . . . the aura will be like a rolling crown. If example is needed, the aura will be a more definite figure, with sharp points and a variety of colors. If the child intends to be a law unto himself, the aura will be like a rolling chain, lower than the position of a crown, going about the shoulders as well as the head."

After learning that, I corralled my son to stand before a white wall so that I could do some aura testing of my own. I have to admit that I didn't have much luck keeping him still so that I could gaze around his little head and shoulders in search of his aura. In fact I had to bribe him with several Oreo cookies. After ten minutes I gave up.

The following day when I picked him up at preschool, his teacher came over and said that when it was Christopher's turn to pick a game for the class to play, he methodically lined up all the kids against the wall and said that it was called "looking for the Oreo"—a game his mother taught him. I guess Oreo cookies and aura are indistinguishable to a five-year-old.

"Our world of comprehension is very small," Cayce continued, referring not to children but adults. "All around us there are colors which we cannot see, just as there are sounds we cannot hear and thoughts we cannot apprehend . . . But if we labor to expand our understanding and consciousness, we can push back the limits a little bit . . . and thus see a little more, understand a little more.''

Pushing Back the Limits

At this point, let's take Cayce's advice and push back the limits of our senses by experimenting with the human energy field or aura. Cayce said that the first step in learning to read auras is simply to observe the colors you and others wear and choose for your everyday surroundings. Once you have practiced this, we'll take the next step.

Hold open your hands a foot apart. Inch by inch draw them toward each other very slowly. When they are about an inch or two apart you probably will be able to feel a sensation of warmth or tingling. This is the energy field of your aura. For some this may feel almost cushionlike. At least that's how it feels in my case. If you can't feel anything, then stop and do Cayce's deep breathing process to release and expand your aura.

Seeing Your Own Aura

Now let's experiment visually with your energy field. Sit before a clean mirror. I usually give mine a once-over with glass cleaner—killing two birds with one stone. The background should be light-colored and solid. A white sheet temporarily propped up behind could do the job nicely. Before you look into the mirror, relax your eyes. Here are two quick and simple methods. Roll your eyes upward until you feel a slight strain, then return them to normal after a few seconds. Another way is to close your eyes very tightly for a few moments. When you open them you'll feel your eye muscles and other facial muscles relax. Do one or both of these exercises several times.

We're ready now to look into the mirror. Gaze several inches above your head and a foot behind you in the mirror. Allow your eyes to go out of focus as you follow the outline of your head and shoulders. Continue to do this for about five minutes. Gradually your peripheral vision will be able to perceive a thin, pulsating line of light emanating from your head and shoulders, perhaps a half-inch wide.

Do you see it? If so, begin to move your head from side to side. Are you following the light? Try taking in a deep breath and releasing it slowly. Were you able to see your aura expand? Now think of a very positive, exalted thought. As you do, keep your eye on the aura. Did that thought make a change in your aura? Positive thoughts are believed to expand the energy field.

Some of you may see colors, although this skill usually comes with more practice. Don't become discouraged if you are not able to see your aura on the first try. Cayce said we all have this ability. It just requires practice. Remember, you are using your vision in a way you're not accustomed to.

Aura Finding with Friends

We'll now experiment with a small group of friends. Stand and form a circle holding hands. Take about a dozen deep, slow breaths. Instruct the group to allow a flow of energy to circulate around the circle. To do this, send the energy down your left arm and out your hand into your partner's right hand. Receive energy from your partner on your right and send it to your partner on your left. Sense this current moving from one person to another. You will feel your energy grow as your aura field expands due to group energy and common positive feelings.

Now break the circle and sit facing a partner. Raise your hands as your partner does the same. Slowly bring the palms of both hands toward your partner's until they are about an inch or so apart and you feel the vibration of your mutual auras.

Keeping your hands in that position, begin to send your partner positive thoughts, either verbally or mentally. As you do, you will be able to move your hands slightly farther apart and still feel the aura.

Now let's place someone from the group in front of a solid, light-colored wall. Gaze at the subject's head and shoulder area using an unfocused stare. I call it the thousand-mile stare. Before you do this, it would be helpful to do the eye exercises to relax you. Maintaining the unfocused stare, you may see the thin, pulsating light surrounding the edge of the head and shoulders. Some people may be able to see colors. For some, depending on how highly developed their perceptions are, the glow may be intense and clearly defined. Notice any variation. Do you all see the same thing? How many are seeing the same colors? Now everyone in the group should send the subject love and positive thoughts at the same time. Did the aura expand? Remember, some might not see this happen on the first try. You have to train your eyes to see the subtle intensity of aura illumination. This ability may vary from subject to subject and from time to time.

Through these experiments there should be palpable evidence that the inner harmonies or discords of a person can be observed and interpreted, reinforcing Cayce's conviction that our every thought has spiritual, mental, and physical impact.

Colors and the Planets: Enter Astrology

You will find in Edgar Cayce's excursions throughout the psychic world that he links and blends many different facets. In regard to his theories on color and auras, he brings in several references to astrology. He notes that the planets themselves reflect certain aspects of color.

To him Mars is the red planet; Mercury, yellow; Saturn, green; Jupiter, blue; Venus, indigo, and so on. Although the sun is not a planet, it carries the connotation of orange. He finds that the planets often have conflicting or opposite influences. The same is true with colors, depending on the circumstances.

Cayce's thoughts on astrology often differ radically from other people's ideas. At times he agrees with the general concepts. He, however, tends to be firmer than the conventional astrologer about the importance of the human will. This has far more importance than the influence of the planets, he said. "The strongest force used in the destiny of man is the sun first, then the closer planets to the earth, or those that are coming to ascension at the time of the birth of the individual, but let it be understood here, no action of any planet, or the phases of the sun, the moon or any of the heavenly bodies surpass the rule of man's willpower" (3744–3).

Since we are involved with the long journey of the soul down through the ages, Cayce did not attach much importance to the astrological conditions at the time of any one particular birth for a sojourn to earth. His scope covers a much larger canvas. The soul is ageless. It exists on different planes of existence, not merely the earthly incarnations. It goes through a constant learning process and is not bound to the earth alone, and has several interims both on the material world and in discarnate experiences between lives.

All through this, the soul is evolving, accumulating data on its Akashic records, revealing its karma, which the sleeping Cayce was able to read. His conclusions disagreed often with conventional astrological charts. He indicated for one correspondent, "Some [of my findings] are in keeping with the astrological charts, others are found to be partially so, others are diametrically opposed to same—because of activities of individuals" (5753–3). He added that much depends on what individuals have done with their urges through incarnations. Commenting further, he said, "The individuality is the sum total of what the entity has done about those things that are creative or ideal in its varied experiences in the earth" (5398–1).

In between earthly visits, the soul may encounter the vibrations of various planets, each of which may produce urges that emerge in a lifetime. Cayce said: "Not that an entity may have manifested physically on such planets, but in that consciousness which is the consciousness of that environ. And these [consciousnesses] have been accredited with certain potential influences in the mental aspect of an entity" (2144–1).

Astrology and Free Will

Cayce was intent on reminding us that while the planets may stir up certain urges within us, they are not the controlling factor: "While there are those urges [from the planets], those urges latent and manifested, know that no urge surpasses the will of the entity—that birthright given each soul that it may know itself to be itself, and by choice becomes one with the Creator. . . . For each soul, each entity is a co-creator with the universal consciousness . . .'' (2571–1).

We can't sit back and blame everything on the stars and planets. Cayce stated bluntly: ''Rather, then, than the stars ruling the life, the life should rule the stars'' (5–2). He indicated also that these planetary urges are not compelling forces, but rather warnings and suggestions as to what to embrace in looking for helpful influences, and especially in reaching for creative forces as an ultimate goal.

Astrology as a Steppingstone

Ten years ago I had a most interesting astrological reading in New Delhi, India. It was given by a locally prominent Hindu astrologer, J. N. Sharma. Sharma combined astrology and palmistry because he felt astrology alone could not determine an individual's total life experience. In fact, his beliefs paralleled Cayce's. One of the first things Sharma told me was ''Fools are ruled by the stars. Wise men control them.'' Like Cayce, Sharma believed that the purpose of astrology should be to make individuals aware that they can adjust their lives to astrological influences. ''Use such directions [from the planets] as steppingstones,'' Cayce said, adding, ''Do not let them become stumbling stones'' (815–6).

I sat before Sharma, cross-legged on the floor of his tiny studio on the outskirts of New Delhi. The only information he knew was my name and the date, time, and place of my birth. Hunched over a small brass table, Sharma sketched my astrological chart on a sheet of brown paper. After that he took my palm in his hand and began to study its lines. Occasionally he would consult his chart. A few moments later he said, "You will always be in a hurry. That is your general temperament."

I was glad that John wasn't around to confirm that. John claims that living with me is like living with the Road Runner out of a Bugs Bunny cartoon.

"Why do you say that?" I asked. I tried to affect a laid-back appearance.

"Because your moon and Saturn are very close together," he said.

I didn't want to appear totally ignorant of astrology, so I just nodded as if it all made perfect sense.

"The field you will adopt is literary," he said, glancing from my palm to my chart. "Writing will be most important because of Mercury's influence. There is also a good deal of Venus here too," he added. "All this combines to point up that you will write very much in your life."

I was startled by what he had said. But I tried not to show it. I didn't want to give him any clues. I quickly tried to figure out if there were any way he could have known that I was a writer. I had arrived at his studio unannounced. No one had referred me.

"Now I must warn you about a health problem. You have low blood pressure," he said. "In later years—after the age of forty-six—this may cause some problems. But not major ones. You should be aware of this condition."

I was aware of the problem. Each time I go for a checkup the nurse has to wrap the large black Velcro band around my upper arm at least two or three times to get a blood pressure reading.

"The age of twenty-seven was a year of changes," he said. "Many changes."

I nodded in agreement. I didn't offer any additional information, but at twenty-seven I met John and quit my job as a flight attendant.

"At the present moment," he continued, "you are having a Saturn phase. This phase will be over on March second—nine days from now. On this date your professional activities will start to shine."

What I didn't know at the time of the reading was that exactly nine days later, the discarnate Benjamin Franklin would make himself known in the tent in the Himalayas and provide me with over a hundred proverbs.

Studying the lines on my palm, Sharma asked, "Who is the man in your life with the initial J?"

"That's my husband," I said. "His name is John."

"You are often insecure," he said. His dark eyes were penetrating. I felt as if he were looking past my eyes into my depths.

"You have the ability to go into deep meditations," he said. "It is during these times that you are replenished creatively. You can easily tune out the outside world. This is very helpful in your writing work. It is also very healthful."

One question I did not want answered was how long I would live. But he told me anyway. "You will live to be seventy-seven years, with no major illness in your life."

I was grateful when he told me that I would live to be seventy-seven. It helped me get up the courage on our Himalayan trek to cross those swinging bamboo bridges. I figured that when I was seventy-six, I could always go see another astrologer.

"You will have difficulty in childbirth," he said.

I was relieved John wasn't around to hear anything to do with babies. John already had three grown sons. In John's own words: "The last thing I need is a new little rug rat tugging at my typewriter ribbon. No peace. No travel. No quiet. And besides that, when I drive the kid to first grade I'll be eighty-five years old!"

When the reading was over, Sharma asked if I had any questions. I asked him if I was really going to have a baby. After a few minutes of consulting my palm and chart, he said: "You'll have a son."

"When?" I asked.

"In three years," he told me.

Christopher was born three years and two months after my visit to Sharma. There was difficulty in the childbirth. As mentioned earlier, he was born six weeks premature with underdeveloped lungs. Fortunately he turned out fine.

Sharma was a good astrologer, but he was a better psychic. Sharma used the astrological chart and palm as tools for his own psychic interpretation. Like Cayce, he was able to dip into the cosmic pool and retrieve information from the past, present, and future, something we all have the ability to do.

We can all be our own best astrologers. Think of your birth sign as a road sign. And think of your psychic ability as your car. Our stars cannot rule us. They can only light the way, guiding us upward and onward in our quest to become One with the Universal Force.

9

DIET, HEALTH, AND HUMOR

Good Health Makes a Good Psychic

Since Cayce regarded the body, mind, and soul as One, he considers care of the body as critical in developing all of these aspects. He reminded us often that the body is the temple of the soul and of God Himself. Although the psychic is beyond the five ordinary senses, the body still acts as a vehicle to carry and house all the psychic actions and information. That is why we must take care of it.

It was Cayce's own giant psychic ability that enabled him to serve thousands of suffering people by pinpointing the causes of their illnesses and showing how they could surmount their physical and mental problems. Now, after fifty years, we know that Cayce was not only effective but far ahead of his time.

Cayce forecast the importance of holistic health and healing, which are now coming into prominence. Some of his

NOTE: As with any folk medicine or over-the-counter drugstore remedies, none of Cayce's suggestions should be used without consultation with your doctor.

cures for "incurable diseases" have been dramatic in succeeding where all conventional medicine had failed. Many of his cures were similar to folk medicine. His diet recommendations were equally folksy, but effective. He was emphatic in insisting that a healthy balanced diet could improve psychic awareness while it improves the bodily functions: "The psychic, then, is of the soul, and it operates through faculties of perception, whether hearing, seeing, feeling, or any portions of the sensory system" (5752–1). He went on to say that these portions of the sensory system depend on our health and our health depends on our diet, exercise, and the way we take care of ourselves.

Cayce was simply suggesting that good health makes for good psychic development. He pointed out that the physical state of our being emerges not only from what we eat but from what we think—what we digest mentally and spiritually. He understood the influences of mental attitudes on physical health long before psychosomatic medicine became important.

Beyond the usual diet recommendations from dieticians, Cayce explored the way we eat and our mental attitudes toward it. We must beware of eating when the body is worried or under any general strain. "Never when under strain, very tired, very excited, or very mad, should the body take foods into the system," he said (137-D-15).

Cayce placed a high value on vegetables, although he was not a strict vegetarian by any means. He indicated that they are a rich source of vitamins, especially the tomato. It is important that vegetables be cooked in their own juices, which in turn should be consumed with the vegetables. An unusual slant is that they should be cooked in Patapar paper. This is a special parchment paper that not only preserves the vegetable juices but holds in the vitamins. It can usually be purchased in health food stores.

As far as minerals go, Cayce had this to say: "Keep

plenty of those foods that supply calcium to the body. These we would find especially in raw carrots, cooked turnips, and turnip greens'' (1968–6). For phosphorus-forming foods, Cayce included carrots, lettuce, shellfish, the peelings of Irish potatoes, and citrus fruit juices.

Balance is important in diet, as with all of Cayce's concepts. Although he leaned toward the alkaline side, he did not rule out some foods that tend to be acidic if an optimal balance is kept in mind. In general, Cayce's approach to a normal diet was one of sound common sense. He did, however, warn against certain food combinations, including some that appear rather harmless, such as citrus fruits and whole-grain cereals. He elaborated on some of these ideas in several readings:

"[The diet] should consist of those foods which will not create too much of an acid nor too much of an alkaline condition throughout the system. It would be better . . . more of the alkaline-producing foods than of the acid-burning foods'' (140-P-50).

He lists alkaline-forming foods as fresh and dried fruits and vegetables, and acid-forming foods as animal fats, vegetable oils, cereal grains, white sugar, nuts, meats, and egg whites. According to Cayce, a normal diet should include about 20 percent acid producers to eighty percent alkaline producers. He said: "In all bodies, the less activity in respect to physical exercise, . . . the greater should be the amount of the alkaline-reacting foods taken. Energies or activities may burn acids; but those who lead a sedentary or nonactive life cannot go on sweets or too many starches. These foods (alkaline- and acid-producing) should be carefully balanced'' (798-P-1).

Cayce also suggested that we include milk products in our diet. He stated: "Milk and all its products should be a portion of the body's diet now; also those food values making for an easy assimilation of iron, silicon, and those elements or chemicals found in all kinds of berries, almost all kinds of vegetables that grow under the ground, almost all of the vegetables of a leafy nature. Fruits and vegetables, nuts and the like should form a greater part of the regular diet'' (480-P-17).

On another point of food combinations, Cayce stressed that orange juice and milk should be taken at opposite ends of the day. He said that if they are taken together, they create drosses or waste matter, which are difficult to eliminate and remain in the system. Cayce added further, ''Have at least one meal each day that includes a quantity of raw vegetables such as cabbage, lettuce, celery, carrots, onions and the like. Tomatoes may be used in their season. Do have plenty of vegetables grown above the ground—at least three of these to one grown below the ground. Have at least one leafy vegetable to every one of the pod vegetables taken (2602-P-1).

In spite of his high regard for vegetables, Cayce still recognized the usefulness of meat protein for body building. His suggestion was: ''Avoid too many heavy meats, not well cooked. . . . Meats taken should preferably be fish, fowl, lamb, others not so often'' (1710-P-3).

He recommended, however, beef juice or broth, plus liver and fish. He warned strongly about grease: ''Keep away from too much grease or too much of any foods cooked in quantities of grease—whether of hog, sheep, beef or fowl! . . . Fish and fowl are the preferred meats. No raw meat, and very little ever of hog meat'' (303–11).

Water, Sleep, and Proper Elimination

The importance of drinking water comes in for its share of attention. Six to eight glasses a day is the suggested quota.

Cayce explained that the water enables the liver and kidneys to function normally, producing the correct elimination of waste from the system. "Always drink plenty of water, before meals and after meals ," Cayce added. "For, as has often been given, when any food value enters the stomach, it immediately becomes a storehouse or a medicine chest that may create all the elements necessary for proper digestion within the system. If foods are first acted upon by pure water, the reactions are more nearly normal. Also, therefore, each morning upon arising, first take a half to three-quarters of a glass of hot water. . . . Not so hot that it is objectionable. Not so tepid that it makes for sickening [reactions], but this will clarify the system of poisons" (311-MS-3).

Cayce brought up many aspects of general health. He insisted that massage and hydrotherapy are good for the body. Hydrotherapy is described in Harold J. Reilly's book *The Edgar Cayce Handbook for Health through Drugless Therapy*. Reilly writes that hydrotherapy is the science of the application of water in all its forms for healing and health. Probably the most common form of hydrotherapy is the steam bath.

"For the hydrotherapy and massage are preventive as well as curative measures," Cayce said, adding, "for the cleansing of the system allows the body forces themselves to function normally, and thus eliminate poisons, congestions and conditions that would become acute through the body" (257–254).

In addition Cayce recommended daily meditation and exercise. "Walking is the best exercise," he said, "but don't take this spasmodically. Have a regular time and do it, rain or shine" (1968–9). Today, forty years later, the American Medical Association's Committee on Exercise and Physical Fitness states: "Walking briskly, not just strolling, is the simplest and also one of the best forms of exercise."

Sleep, according to Cayce, is as important as diet and exercise. He said that sleep is needed for the physical body to draw on the mental and spiritual powers. For those who have trouble falling asleep, Cayce urged a full quota of physical activity during the day, especially if your occupation is sedentary. He also recommended massage or hydro-therapy plus the simple concoction of a warm glass of milk with a little honey stirred in. Furthermore, Cayce was convinced that if we make it a strict point to do one good turn for someone a day, it will have a strong effect on getting a good night's sleep. This bit of advice fits in with his famous statement that when you enter heaven you'll be leaning on someone you have helped. It seems that karma in every form and degree runs through Cayce's work.

Golden Rules for the Body

So thorough has the A.R.E. been in presenting the Cayce record of health advice that it has created a full program on cassette tape to detail the way to better health. It is called *Thirty Days to a Healthier You: Edgar Cayce's Guide to Holistic Health*. The taped program is conducted under the supervision of two physicians, Gladys McGarey, M.D., and her husband, William McGarey, M.D. Their research on the Cayce methods is conducted at the A.R.E. clinic in Phoenix, Arizona, where for the past thirty years they have applied Cayce's nutritional advice and achieved dramatic results. In this taped program, eight basic premises of the Edgar Cayce medical readings have been summarized.

1. We are spiritual beings. The body is the temple of the soul and the dwelling place of the mind.

2. There is a pattern within every system of the body for the proper functioning of the cells of that system.

3. Each part, each structure, each system of the body affects and bears a relationship to the whole.

4. We are responsible for the bodies we have built and are building.

5. Attitudes affect the physical body and do so constructively or destructively.

6. The system is built by assimilation of nutrients and is able to restore itself so long as the eliminations do not hinder the process.

7. Rest and recreation are spiritual, mental, and physical necessities.

8. Application must be persistent and consistent.

The emphasis of this program is not so much the treatment of a diagnosed illness as the maintenance of health and the prevention of illness.

Cayce, Folk Medicine, and Medical Approval

The *Thirty Days to a Healthier You* course reminds me of an editorial in the Journal of the American Medical Association that acknowledged that Cayce was the originator of modern holistic medicine and healing. The March 16, 1979, editorial states: ''The roots of present-day holism probably go back 100 years to the birth of Edgar Cayce in Hopkinsville, Kentucky. By the time he died in 1944, Cayce was well recognized as a mystic who entered sleep trances and dictated a philosophy of life and healing called 'readings.' ''

Some of the Cayce advice was not accepted in his early days, but is now being widely accepted in medical circles. Another important point made in the taped course is that 90 percent of the physical readings Cayce gave were medically confirmed.

Each time Cayce gave a reading, he would follow the same pattern. Lying back on his couch, he would be read the letter from a correspondent and invariably say, ''Yes, we have the body here,'' as if it were there in physical form, even though it could be thousands of miles away. He would also always begin with his analysis of the blood circulation of the correspondent. Then he would trace the functioning of the nervous system, followed by an examination of the organs and how they were functioning. From there he would go to the cause of the trouble and then follow that up with a prescription for the relief of the symptoms. Next and most important he would observe the spiritual problems that might be affecting the body and direct the individual toward spiritual harmony. Cayce believed that the body and the mind must be in harmony before a healing could take place.

All this was miraculously conducted by remote viewing, yet he could see the physical problems as if he were examining an X-ray. Anyone present or absent who was involved in the reading was instructed by Cayce to maintain a prayerful and meditative state. Usually the only two people in the reading room with Cayce were his wife, Gertrude, and secretary, Gladys Turner.

After each reading, Gladys Turner would forward the advice to the person who had requested it. There would be varied reactions. Some people depended completely on the readings and scrupulously followed all advice given by the sleeping Cayce. Others would be skeptical and lack belief, but would take a chance on the recommendations. When they did follow the advice, they almost invariably got helpful results.

The readings stressed the importance of doing everything recommended without the use of other procedures, although at times Cayce would agree with the medical treatments that had been prescribed. In general he would combine the holistic approach with the traditional and thus become a medical adviser and a spiritual guide.

Many of the Cayce folk medicine cures seem strange in this modern age. But the results in most cases were total cures. Quite often he recommended placing packs directly on the body. One of the most interesting is the castor oil pack. In fact it is mentioned so frequently it deserves special attention. Dr. William McGarey wrote in his book *The Edgar Cayce Remedies,* that of all the therapies he has used in the practice of medicine he has never found any that surpasses castor oil in its usefulness, healing qualities, or scope of therapeutic application.

In the Middle Ages castor oil was known as "palma Christi," or the "Palm of Christ," after the plant from which it is obtained. Its usages include treatment for a broad range of afflictions and injuries and even as a tranquilizer. How and why it works is still a mystery. But the successes of Drs. Gladys and William McGarey are so well documented that the picture is rather startling. William McGarey explained that the oil stimulates the lymphatic system while at the same time enhancing the elimination of toxic substances from the cells where the pack is applied locally. When the pack is applied over the lower abdomen for an hour or so, general systemic effects are reported and confirmed. Because of the wide range of use, I'm presenting the method of applying a castor oil pack in detail, as described in the readings:

You will need about four thicknesses of soft flannel folded

to about a ten-by-fourteen-inch rectangle for abdominal use. (The cloth can be shaped to fit local areas depending on the size of the affliction such as a wound, rash, swelling, or laceration.) Saturate the cloth with warm castor oil and squeeze out. Place over the abdomen, cover with a plastic sheet, and then cover with an electric heating pad. All this is to remain in place for an hour to an hour and a half. Suggested use for optimum results is five times a week for a total of twenty to twenty-eight days. While this is not a panacea, its beneficial use in such a broad range of problems makes it well worth experimenting with.

The Cayce treatments and remedies have stood the test of time. Cayce, however, never thought of himself as unique. He believed that many people could accomplish what he did if they listened to the voice within. After Cayce's death, Gladys Turner, his former secretary, listened to her inner voice when she was suffering from digestive trouble. In a dream she heard Cayce tell her to take a special tea, called fennel. It worked perfectly and she had no trouble after that.

Anger and the Glands

An outstanding case in Gladys Turner's memory illustrates graphically how important it is for us to get rid of our hostilities. This is never an easy thing to do since they are often deep seated, yet getting rid of them can be one of the most important things in life. In this case, a woman was suffering from ill health and was dominated by a fierce hatred of her mother-in-law. Cayce suggested that she rid herself of this hatred through regular meditation and prayer. The results were dramatic. Almost overnight she went from poor health to vitality.

Charles Thomas Cayce reminds us how anger and hostility have a very clear physiological effect upon the adrenal glands, creating a syndrome known as "fight response." Meditation has been shown to ameliorate this condition, bringing a relaxation response.

Meditation and Stress

Edgar Cayce believed in the effectiveness of meditation throughout our lives. Charles Thomas joins his grandfather in this conviction. However, when Charles Thomas first began to follow a meditation program it wasn't easy for him to remain committed and enthusiastic. He found all too often that he allowed meditation to get squeezed out of his daily routine. At times he talked himself out of practicing, admitting to pure laziness plus rebellion against investing so much time in it. Like many of us, he asked the question: Does it really work? Today Charles Thomas meditates daily. He knows for a fact that it is the best investment of time we can make for ourselves, especially in the handling of stress. Throughout the A.R.E. health program, Charles Thomas emphasizes the importance that stress reduction plays in maintaining a healthy body.

Utilizing a Holistic Approach

Today there are dozens of doctors who practice Cayce's methods. And there are many others who subscribe to his holistic principles in general without necessarily following his detailed regimen. Dr. Paul G. Epstein, a naturopathic physician, runs the Center for Holistic Medicine in Norwalk, Connecticut, where he uses natural medicines in treating patients and believes, as Cayce did, that healing comes from within the individual.

"My primary job as a physician is to help the patient stimulate his or her own healing energy," Dr. Epstein told me during a recent interview at his center.

"How do you accomplish that?" I asked.

"Our approach is a holistic one. Not only do we take into consideration the physical symptoms, but we also consider the mental, emotional, and psychological factors," Dr. Epstein said, adding, "but I'm not saying that it's inappropriate at times to use first-aid techniques. A lot of people are under the misconception that holistic medicine negates surgery and drugs. That's not the case. We consider all types of health care to facilitate change and healing. It's not an either/or situation. In some cases it might best suit a patient to take a drug along with stress management or guided imagery."

I told Dr. Epstein that Cayce believed that negative emotions such as anger, hate, resentment, and so forth secrete poisons into the lymphatic system that block elimination, deplete energy, and generally create an environment for disease.

"That's right," Dr. Epstein replied. "Physical symptoms are often manifestations of imbalances on different levels. Unfortunately our whole health care system today has been set up to fix only the manifestation. Cut it out. Take a drug. Suppress the symptom. What I'm talking about is getting deeper than the symptoms and treating the underlying causes. Maybe it's getting the patient to deal with deep emotional conflicts. The patient must participate in his or her own healing. A good example of this is Norman Cousins' book *The Anatomy of an Illness*. Cousins' story of chronic illness illustrates the value of personal responsibility and deciding to get well as opposed to waiting for the doctor or the medicines to help you. Real healing comes from within."

"So you're saying that healing means opening yourself

up to the natural forces within?" I asked.

"Yes," Dr. Epstein replied, "changing the attitudes and beliefs that limit your ability to become healthy. True health is not merely an absence of disease, it's a state of optimal function."

"Cayce said that even the common cold required mental and emotional change," I said.

"That's true," Dr. Epstein said. "If a patient comes to me with a chronic sore throat, I want to get to the root of the problem rather than just merely alleviate the symptom. I want my patient to be able to get involved in the healing process, and not just on one level. We're talking about the mind, body, spirit, emotions—the whole being becomes involved in the healing process. What we're doing is trying to find the proper balance and allow the body to heal itself."

"And you do this with natural therapies?" I asked.

"Yes," he said. "We use vitamins, minerals, herbs, nutrition, stress management, exercise therapy, life-style counseling, and so on."

Dr. Epstein went on to say that illness can often be a positive force in your life. It can be an opportunity for growth. Illness is showing us that something is wrong at a much deeper level. For instance, he says, the root cause might be stress.

"The Academy of Family Physicians stated in a recent journal that something like two-thirds of all office visits to the family doctor are stress related," Dr. Epstein said. "We're not taught in this culture to take responsibility for our own health. And that's too bad because as Albert Schweitzer said: 'Each person carries his own doctor inside him.' The patient is at his best when he gives the doctor that resides in him a chance to go to work."

How does Dr. Epstein suggest we put this doctor inside of us to work? He recommends a technique known as "guided imagery." He believes it is an invaluable tool for contacting one's self at deeper levels of consciousness. He explains the process as a means of expression of the unconscious mind. To Dr. Epstein, guided imagery acts as a bridge between the conscious and the unconscious mind.

"I think a key point to make here is that guided imagery works not just because Edgar Cayce said so in a reading, which is true, but because recent scientific data suggests a direct link between the mind and the immune system," Dr. Epstein said, adding, "This newly emerging field is called psychoneuroimmunology."

Dr. Epstein believes that through guided imagery an individual can bring out both the intuitive and the creative forces. These can strengthen the immune system and promote self-healing. The technique has been found particularly helpful in cases of hypertension, asthma, arthritis, migraines, allergies, emotional disturbance, and stress-related disorders.

An Exercise in Guided Imagery

Let's put this doctor inside of us in action. There are several visualization exercises to promote healing by guided imagery. For one exercise we'll start with a relaxation technique suggested in the Cayce material: Take a deep breath through the nose with the mouth closed. As you breathe in, think the phrase: "I am calm." Hold the breath for a few moments and slowly exhale through your mouth and think: "I am serene." Repeat this over and over.

A form of autosuggestion will aid in further relaxation. Tense the muscles from head to toe one at a time. Repeat to yourself: "I tense the muscles in my scalp. Now I let go, and relax deeper. I tense the muscles in my forehead. Now I let go and relax deeper. . . ." Continue tensing and relaxing and repeating this phrase as you move down through the muscle system in the body. This is, of course, simply the reverse of the toes-to-head relaxation method described earlier. The repeating of "Now I let go and relax deeper" is important. Finally, as you do so, say, "I tense the muscles of my entire body. Now I let go and relax deeper."

Now that you are physically relaxed, go to a place in your mind where you feel most at peace. Perhaps it's a country scene on a sunny day, or the ocean at sunset with a cool breeze sweeping over you, or a verdant woodland at dawn. Once you are in your special place, imagine a beam of white light coming through the top of your head, bringing a tingling sensation as the warmth of the light flows through you. Visualize this healing white light circulating through your entire body, rinsing every cell, bathing you in its healing energy. Now direct this brilliant beam of white energy to the specific troubled area. Imagine it penetrating the area and slowly dissolving everything negative.

You may want to call in your spirit guides to lend additional healing energy. Remember, they are here for you if only you ask. Feel their energy encompassing you in healing love, protecting you from negative forces. Perhaps you would like to ask if they have a message concerning your particular problem. Maybe they can supply you with insight into the underlying causes.

Now be still and listen for the answer. It might be symbolic. It might be literal. Whatever the case, it is important that you open yourself up to receiving the answer. Don't be discouraged if you fail to receive an immediate answer. Often answers come like flashes of lightning at the most unexpected times. But be confident that an answer will come.

After twenty or thirty minutes, close your visualization by picturing yourself vibrant and radiant and in the glow of the Divine Creative Forces. Know that the doctor within you has begun to restore you to perfect health.

You may want to reflect on this affirmation of Edgar Cayce's:

"Know that all strength, all healing of every nature is the changing of the vibrations from within—the attuning of the divine within the living tissue of a body to Creative Energies. This alone is healing"(3370–1).

Perhaps in your meditations some affirmations of your own may come which may be helpful to your specific needs. The following affirmations emerged from my meditations and have been of help to me.

I am opening all the cells of my body to the Divine Healing Energy that I draw in with each breath as I exhale all negative thoughts and feelings.

I release myself into the infinite Pool of Universal Energy. I feel it flood my body and mind with new and creative energy of its own.

In opening myself to the Divine inflow I feel the denseness of the material world fading and feel buoyant as I become more in harmony with the Creative Forces.

Group Effort

Since Cayce believed that a group effort reinforces the healing process, let's try it now. Stand with your friends and form a circle holding hands. Instruct the group to take a deep breath through the nose, hold the breath for a count of five, and exhale slowly through the mouth. Imagine every cell in your body being flooded with a Divine inflow of healing energy. Picture the energy flowing down your arm and into the hand of the person on your right so that the energy moves around the circle. Form an image of any disturbed areas and picture the healing energy rinsing every cell and particle of them. As the healing energy from the circle enters your left arm, send it out again with a new pulsation.

Continue this process for fifteen minutes or so, ending with a brief mantra like the Buddhist's "Om Mani Padme Aum," or simply just an extended "Hum," visualizing yourself in harmony with the vibrations of the Universe.

At the end of the session you may stretch to bring yourself back to your normal consciousness. In fact, Cayce suggested that stretching the way a cat does is an effective way of relaxing.

The Importance of Humor

There is no way to speak of health without bringing up the importance of humor in maintaining a fit body. A favorite theme of Cayce's life readings was that a sense of humor is a balance wheel for our emotions. He believed firmly that humor could ease life's burdens and help point our attitude in a positive and joyful direction for this lifetime and future lifetimes. Cayce expressed this thought in the following reading: "The entity should attempt seriously, prayerfully, spiritually to see even that as might be called the ridiculous side of every question. Remember that a good laugh, an arousing even to what might in some be called hilariousness, is good for the body physically, mentally, and gives the opportunity for the greater mental and spiritual awakening" (2647–1).

Once again Cayce was fifty years ahead of his time. In the *New York Times* of August 4, 1987, Dr. Alice M. Isen, a psychologist at the University of Maryland, was reported to have conducted research that concretely demonstrates the positive effects of humor. She writes that any joke that makes you feel good is likely to help you think more broadly and creatively. Dr. Isen has found that the elation from hearing a good joke is similar to that which people feel when they receive a small, unexpected gift. Her research shows that such elation facilitates creativity.

A recent issue of the *Journal of Personality and Social Psychology* reported that Dr. Isen found that individuals who had just watched a comedy film of television "bloopers" were better able to find a creative solution to a puzzling problem than those who had watched a film about math or had exercised.

Edgar Cayce put it this way: "Smile and laugh often. Seek to find and read those things that are of a humorous nature, rather than those that are morose" (1306–2).

Hugh Lynn Cayce wrote that individuals who were bright and witty appealed to his father. He delighted in their joyful spirit. In his trance state he advised them to keep their humor: "Do *not* lose this sense of humor," Cayce said. "It will oft be a means for saving many an unseeming situation" (2421–2).

10

OVERALL PERSPECTIVE

A Total Commitment

By now it must be evident that psychic development is a total commitment to search deep within yourself in order to discover the purpose of your higher self. Think of this as a quest. You are about to receive a Celestial Doctorate in knowing yourself. Through this quest you begin to "see" yourself the way you really are—not the way others tell you you are. In turn you will "see" others the way they really are. You will find yourself releasing control of and expectations for those close to you. You will find fear, negativity, and hostility replaced by love and compassion as you strive to make contact with the Universal Force or the Oneness of life.

Beyond the Finite Mind

You will be able to free yourself from the bondage of your finite mind, which has kept you bound in frustrating confinement. You will explore the unique gifts that you have held in cold storage from this lifetime and past lifetimes. Ultimately you will apply everything you have discovered about yourself to enhance the quality of your relationships, career, health, finances, and, of course, your spiritual life. The rewards are virtually limitless. The deeper you dig, the higher you will reach.

If all this sounds too much like hype, it isn't. These exalted benefits have been documented in the more than fourteen thousand Edgar Cayce readings. Literally thousands of lives have been changed by following Cayce's advice. Cayce said that our first job is to trust in the spiritual. It is this trust that does more to stimulate psychic ability than anything else. Cayce was quick to add that worries about material life can block your development.

Nobody is suggesting that you have to turn in your B.M.W., hot tub, and Wedgwood for a camel, bucket, and begging bowl in order to search for your spiritual riches. That's not the point. The point is that you become balanced, spiritually, mentally, and materially. For the last fifty years or so, advertising executives on Madison Avenue have ruled the country with an iron fist wrapped in a Gucci glove. According to them, the self within is without substance. The sad fact is that many of us are on a Madison Avenue roller coaster that whips us through the Shopping Malls of Life. Already my saucy scamp of a son expects to be chauffeured to a string of different stores in search of the latest designer jeans. As I dutifully pass the sales clerk my credit card I think: How can a five-year-old be so shallow and superficial when he has a mother who is dedicated to spiritual upliftment?

I must add, however, that before my spiritual quest began fifteen years ago, my values made those of Zsa Zsa Gabor seem like those of Mother Teresa. My compulsive need to live in the fast lane was a direct result of a boxing match between my repressed spiritual nature and my active material nature. My spiritual side wanted equal time and I was telling it to take a hike.

Since we are spiritual beings, this side of us must manifest itself or turmoil will take over. Because of our society, constant effort is required to maintain a balance. Television, magazines, newspapers, and movies blast us with the message: If you want to be happy, you must be upwardly mobile. Cayce believed the same thing. But for Cayce upwardly mobile meant reaching toward the Universal Force.

Finding Peace Within

Our biggest job and top priority is to find peace within. This isn't easy in a turbulent world that is churning with hostility and discontent. Cayce stands head and shoulders above the other great psychics; his readings face this challenge and attack with vigor.

In my long exploration of Cayce's works, several signposts stand out. Cayce may have been repetitious in helping us to probe the Universe, but I think he was repetitious for the sake of emphasis. Like a pro tennis player he drives ball after ball with confidence and speed to try to get his message through. If we are able to find inner peace, we are far better able to release our consciousness beyond the five senses, which is the object of our attempt to use our psychic senses.

Just how do we go about discovering this inner peace? We all are in a river of life. It's an angry river of boiling waters, with a swift churning current sweeping us toward an unseen sea full of rocks and boulders to smash against. We have to accept that we're in this river whether we like it or not. The current is so swift we can't swim back against it. We can't swim toward the nearest shore. We can't get out of our situation, so we may as well at least try to steer. This is where Cayce's emphasis on free will comes in. He believed free will can save us.

A close friend of mine once went to a capable psychic who reluctantly foresaw an automobile accident coming up in his life. The psychic told my friend that extra caution could help the situation even though the forecast seemed to be inevitable.

Several months later while driving he noticed that the road was suddenly becoming slippery, although this was not obvious. He slowed and cautiously applied his brakes. As he did, a car suddenly skidded out into his lane and crashed into him with a glancing blow. All were safe. This was a healthy use of precognition to tame fate in what could have been a fatal situation.

This incident illustrates Cayce's underlying thought: Temper the exigencies of fate by using your free will to alter its harmful consequences. But the foundation of all of Cayce's convictions can be illustrated by returning to the analogy of the dangerous river of life. Suppose your rubber raft was being catapulted toward Niagara Falls with no way for you to stop it. A rescue helicopter comes overhead and drops a cable that you can grab to be safely hauled up to the craft. You use it because it is the one thing that can pull you above the turbulence. This is what Cayce meant when he advised us to reach upward to the highest Creative Forces of the Universe. They are a safety cable far above our limited resources. Reach upward and grab them, said Cayce, and the turbulent waters sweeping you toward the waterfall lose their power over you.

While working with my husband, John, in the Italian-Swiss Alps on a documentary film for NBC, we saw this metaphor come vividly to life as a Swiss Air Rescue helicopter plucked two stranded mountain climbers from a precarious ledge.

It was a harrowing adventure with an interesting psychic twist. The two climbers were stranded on a six-inch ledge on the steep face of the mountain known as Piz Badile. They were secured only by ropes anchored to pitons driven into the iced and slippery granite face. As night approached, snow and freezing rain encased the mountain and the climbers with a crust of ice. Beneath their ledge was a sheer drop of two thousand feet. All they could do to keep from freezing was to wriggle their toes. Any other movement would leave them hanging free. They clung to their perch for three freezing days and nights with the mountain encased in fog, which made it impossible for the Swiss Air helicopter crew to fly.

Several times they were ready to give up. Just as one man decided to do so, he felt himself leaving his body. It was as if he floated out into space to look back at his own body. He was suddenly filled with a spiritual light that gave him courage to hold on and to secure his companion also.

On the fourth day, the helicopter arrived. It hovered less than twenty feet from the wall of the mountain and dropped the rescue cable. To reach it, the climber who had had the out-of-body experience had to unhook himself from the piton and reach out. He did so with superhuman effort and was lifted off to safety. His companion was rescued afterward.

The situation was illustrative of Cayce's premise that to reach upward to the higher sources, we have to unhook ourselves from our material bondage and reach up for comfort and safety.

Meditation: A Daily Routine

Meditation is the fundamental and essential tool to opening the doors to our higher reality. Cayce said that we must learn to meditate just as we have learned to walk and talk. He added that in order for meditation to be truly effective it must be done each day.

I have found Cayce's admonition to BE STILL! to be a great way to get into the daily meditative state. This seems a simple enough step, but it can be so hard to come to that screeching halt in a day's routine that special effort is required. As I mentioned, I meditate at the same time each day—another one of Cayce's recommendations. I make a point to never miss even one day for fear that will break the pattern. In fact, I've managed to trick myself into believing that at 9:30 A.M. the Meditation Train pulls away with my office, sofa in tow. Since I've always been somewhat neurotic about missing any train, bus, or plane, I'm on my sofa by 9:29, clearing my mind of all negative thoughts and all the day's distractions.

The Selfless Prayer

On the subject of negative thoughts, Cayce once again drove home the point that our first task is to search within, removing all hate, resentment, and hostility. He said that conflicts with anyone must be resolved or we will not connect with the Universal Oneness. Cayce acknowledged that many of us may have difficulty with this and offered the prayer of "Loving Indifference" to help us forgive someone we feel has wronged us: "Lord, he is Thine, even as I am

Thine. Do that which will bring peace and harmony between us.''

Cayce believed this prayer was beneficial because it does not place the blame on the other party or set ourselves up as paragons of virtue. The prayer simply asks for peace and harmony to overcome resentments.

I often use this prayer when I feel negativity stalking my thoughts. The other day, for instance, I met a friend on the street. During our brief conversation she asked how I was doing. I told her that I had been extremely busy, taking care of Christopher, writing, and keeping up with household chores. She replied: "Well, a clean house was never one of your priorities."

I walked away feeling hostility bubbling up like a witch's brew. By the time I got home I had drummed up a variety of insults to even the score. At the same time I felt sapped of energy. Tension had caused my muscles to ache and my head to pound. My body was telling me to "give it up." I heeded the warning, sat down, and said the Cayce prayer. As I did, I could actually feel my hostility dissipating, as if air were escaping from a balloon. Moments later I was relaxed, refreshed, and had plenty of energy even to clean my house.

The Psychic and Religion

Love and compassion are as basic to Cayce as a hammer and nail are to a carpenter. In fact, love and compassion are Cayce's building blocks. "Do not belittle. Do not hate," he said in reading 1537–1. "For hate CREATES as does Love. . . . Love one another and thus fulfill the law of God, for God is Love."

From this and nearly all of the readings, we come to the

inescapable conclusion that we can't dip into the psychic without getting into religion, but not religion in the conventional sense of the word. The word religion simply means to re-bind. And that is how Cayce thought of religion—re-binding with the Universal Force that put us here in the first place.

Paralleling Edgar Cayce's deep religious convictions are those of Ralph Waldo Trine, whose book *In Tune with the Infinite* reinforces much of what Cayce said. Trine says that when the spiritual sense is opened, it transcends all the limitations of our physical senses and intellect. Trine comments further that we can be at one with the Infinite Life if we listen to our inner voice, and as a result we will always have Divine illumination and guidance. Trine indicates that this will enable us to live in heaven here and now, today and every day.

Cayce agreed with this here-and-now concept. It attracted me to Edgar Cayce. He presented a religious viewpoint that embraces all the world without the provincialism that says: This is an exclusive club; anybody who doesn't join us is out of the picture. Since this attitude excludes so much of the world's population, I find it hard to accept.

I didn't always find it hard to accept. As an impressionable youth in parochial school, I had no doubt that only Catholics would be lounging around Heaven eating TV dinners and watching Bishop Fulton J. Sheen every Sunday night. This belief was a direct result of what we were taught. We were the Chosen People. In fact we weren't even allowed to set foot into any church other than a Catholic church. To do so was a mortal sin.

In spite of Cayce's ecumenical view, it must be recognized that he was anchored to what he calls the "Christ Consciousness." Cayce offered a fresh and invigorating picture of Him and suggests in effect that Christianity in its organized form unfortunately can distort the real meaning and spirit of Christ. He believed this was the result of fallible people setting up an exclusivity that Christ never intended.

Edgar Cayce's views were not limited to the Judeo-Christian context. Cayce believed that Jesus was an entity influenced directly or indirectly by all forms of philosophy or religious thought that taught that God was One. Cayce asserted that the influence on the earth from the spirit world added much to Confucianism, Buddhism, Platonism, and other systems of belief. Cayce also said that the ''Christ Consciousness'' lies in all men as man's spiritual nature. It is awakened by turning the human will over to the will of God and becoming One with God.

Seeing Through the Clouds

How do we summarize such a multifaceted man as Edgar Cayce? He explored every corner of the Universe, the subconscious, the conscious, and the human soul. Yet his basic premise boils down to an all-inclusive Oneness, reflecting the conclusion that ALL is ONE.

However, this doesn't mean that we can't examine the particles to see how they converge in his ultimate conclusion. In fact, each of these varied particles of the psychic has its own benefits. Channeling produces powerful evidence that life is continuous. Reincarnation suggests that we have the opportunity to learn from the past to make this life richer. The existence of spirit guides demonstrates that we have assistance waiting for us here and now if only we ask. Dreams are a window to our unconscious and provide a vehicle for exploring and understanding our life's purpose. Psychometry, remote viewing, and telepathy are tools that help us extend our five senses to realize a much greater reality. Auras are the outward reflection of the vital energies within that reveal our spiritual and physical condition. Diet and health form a bridge from the solid, material world of the body into the world of the psychic. And humor, Cayce told us, can ease life's burdens and help point our attitude in a positive and joyful direction.

All these particles combine to shape a picture of the giant psychic balloon that expands to go beyond the five senses. I have been able to experience phenomena that go far beyond what my limited senses could perceive. I am in full agreement with Cayce: The psychic is latent within all of us.

Practicing psychic abilities for the sake of theatrical display reduces the phenomena to the category of parlor games. The real goal, as Cayce repeated constantly, is to illustrate that each of us has the capacity to reach an attunement with the Creative Forces of the Universe for a more constructive life. But I doubt if I would have been able to comprehend the infinite canvas of Edgar Cayce without my own experiences in the psychic world. Each experience serves as a glimpse through a crack in the clouds.

How do these peeks through the clouds and my in-depth exploration of Edgar Cayce's work help me? I used to wake up in the morning with an underlying sense of guilt. I felt as if I weren't doing enough to justify my existence. Part of me wanted to give all of our worldly belongings to the less fortunate. The other part of me wanted to buy a second home in Aspen. When I told this to John, he admitted that daily he had vague, floating thoughts of joining the Peace Corps in order to justify his being here. But he also has thoughts of a trim forty-five-foot sloop with a hefty auxiliary engine and nylon sails.

I hate to speculate on how Freud might have analyzed us. But I do know what Cayce would have said. We were feeling an underlying sense of guilt because we were not operating at our highest level. Our spiritual and physical natures were out of synch with the Creative Forces. This resulted in inner turmoil.

Ever since I made a conscious effort to follow Cayce's program of development, I've gained a healthier view of the world and the greater reality beyond it. Although I had been involved in the psychic long before I studied Cayce, Cayce seemed to hook it all together for me. My physical and spiritual nature are in balance. I now have a sense of peace that permeates even my most frazzled days. In the past I used to have a nagging fear of getting old and sick and dying. I did everything but read the obituary column to make sure I wasn't in it. This doesn't mean, however, that since I have lost my fear of death I will throw caution to the wind. I'm still a bit reluctant to get in a car if my brother is at the wheel.

Furthermore, I've come to regard myself as a unique individual with a specific purpose and constructive goals to aim for. I no longer feel I have to be an astrophysicist or an M.I.T. microbiologist to be important. I no longer tote around every negative word that has ever been thrown my way. My days as an injustice collector are history. I have found the pearl in myself. And I have found it in others.

There is no question that Cayce's teachings have altered my life. I'm confident that if you follow the steps outlined in this book you too will find a similar peace as you join Cayce in his metaphysical outreach to the near and far corners of the Universe. You will find yourself rising above the fog of everyday living to discover a fixed star that will keep you on a safe and constant course to fu fillment.

ACKNOWLEDGMENTS

I would like to thank all the A.R.E. staff members for the magnificent help they gave me in writing this book. I would like to add special thanks to Jeanette Thomas, Robert Jeffries, and Charles Thomas Cayce, who went above and beyond the call of duty in giving me help and encouragement.

INDEX